GOD'S Story

FROM THE BEGINNING TO THE PROMISED RETURN

Stories retold by Becki Dudley

First printing: May 2023

Master Books, P.O. Box 726, Green Forest, AR 72638

Master Books® is a division of the New Leaf Publishing Group, LLC

ISBN: 978-1-68344-288-2

ISBN: 978-1-61458-805-4 (digital)

Library of Congress Control Number: 2023933064

Interior and Cover design by Diana Bogardus

Please consider requesting that a copy of this volume be purchased by your local library system.

Printed in China

Please visit our website for other great titles: www.masterbooks.com

For information regarding promotional opportunities, please contact the publicity department at pr@nlpg.com.

Before you read this book...

"In the Old Testament the New is concealed, in the New the Old is revealed."

—St. Augustine

While in place from the beginning, God's redemptive plan for mankind was revealed over the course of time. It is in that light that the stories in this book are presented. The reader will get a small glimpse into the lives, times, and cultures of the people whose stories are told, some of whom lived thousands of years before Jesus — long before an understanding of His life and purpose were fully understood. So as you engage with this story, keep in mind that the narrative builds to a climax, just as it does in the Bible.

The stories have been paraphrased by the author. However, direct Scripture quotes are often used, having been included for the clarity and authority of God's Word. These are italicized, with biblical references, throughout the book.

This is not an exhaustive retelling or commentary on the Bible in its entirety, but rather a selection of stories from God's Word that highlight His redemptive plan for a fallen world.

Special Features:

- Section summaries entitled *Threads of Hope* are included to help tie the story together

- Helpful definitions at the end of each section

- Designed for families and individuals of all ages; includes simple summaries for younger readers

- Beautiful illustrations and maps.

- Scripture references for each story

It is the author's hope that this book will remind you of God's goodness, faithfulness, and His sacrifice for us. May you, your family, and your faith be blessed by *God's Story*.

Look for the summaries for younger readers. Quick and easy to read, they present each story in a simple way to engage a child's interest.

Table of Contents: Part One

Preface

We live in a world of wonder and beauty. Full of stars and planets, animals and people, flowers, trees, oceans, and so much more! But as amazing as these things are, none have the power to create themselves out of nothing. You see, in time past, the universe as we know it did not exist. It all began when God chose to create. With power and creativity, He spoke the natural world into existence.

It is hard for us to comprehend that kind of power.

God is a supernatural being. He is eternal, not created, having no beginning or end. God exists in three persons: Father, Son, and Holy Spirit. They co-exist and work together as one and are known as the Trinity. The prophet Isaiah had a vision that gives us a tiny glimpse of God's greatness:

In the year that King Uzziah died I saw the Lord sitting upon a throne, high and lifted up; and the train of his robe filled the temple. Above him stood the seraphim. Each had six wings: with two he covered his face, and with two he covered his feet, and with two he flew. And one called to another and said: "Holy, holy, holy is the Lord of hosts; the whole earth is full of his glory!" (Isaiah 6:1–3)

To be holy is to be absolutely good and pure. God does not choose to act in a way that is good and pure — His very being is good and sinless. He cannot think or act or be anything other than good. This is what sets Him apart from everything else that exists. This is also why He must stand against that which is not good.

Mankind is unable to fully understand God, but thankfully the Bible teaches us enough about Him to understand what we need to know. The word **Bible** comes from the Greek word *biblia*, which means "books." The Bible is a collection of many different books, similar to a library. This collection includes different genres, such as history, poetry, and prophecy. The words in these books were inspired by the Holy Spirit of God (2 Timothy 3:16), which explains why the Bible is known as *God's Word*. When put together, all these books tell ***God's Story***.

The best way to understand the Bible is to read and study the whole collection again and again over your lifetime. It is the best-selling book of all time. It has been printed in hundreds of languages and is loved the world over. While the Bible may be ancient, it never gets old! Its words are as true and powerful today as they were a thousand years ago.

This book is just a small sample of the Bible's riches. It highlights the big story of the Bible — God's redemptive plan in response to the sin and fall of mankind.

Redemption is the main theme that weaves its way throughout this story, from the Garden of Eden to the Cross of Christ. This has often been referred to as the *scarlet thread of redemption*.

We hope you enjoy this miraculous, true story.

Part One:
Of Darkness and Light

*A*battle wages on the earth today, at least as old as the ground upon which we walk. It began when an angelic being challenged the one true God.

This being is commonly referred to as Satan in the Bible. However, there are many passages that assign other names to him. The evil one, the devil, the father of lies, the adversary, dragon, serpent, and ruler of the world are a few of them. These names give an apt description of his character. He is evil.

Satan was created by God and was a high-ranking guardian cherub. He was uniquely beautiful. His heart became proud, and he fancied himself God's equal. He turned on his Creator and began the very long war against God.

Satan has a certain amount of power and uses it in an attempt to turn people away from God. Satan is clever and often works in the shadows. He is also a master of disguise and can pretend to be an angel of light. Thankfully, he is not as powerful as God.

God has chosen to allow Satan to have influence over this world for a time. We may not understand God's reasons for this, but we can trust in His wisdom. At the very least, by allowing Satan to influence the earth, people will have the opportunity to understand for themselves the true nature of God and His enemy, of good and of evil.

As you read *God's Story*, you will learn that Satan's fate has already been decided. One day in the future he will be destroyed for good, and evil will no longer exist. Until then, we would do well to remember that he is an enemy of God and mankind.

Satan entices people to sin but cannot force anyone to do anything. God has given people free will to make their own decisions. Thankfully, God also understands our human weaknesses and has made forgiveness and restoration possible. Much will be said about this as you read through this redemptive story, which culminates on a cross outside of Jerusalem.

The contrast between God and Satan, between darkness and light, could not be more clear. One seeks to give life and abundance, and the other to bring death and destruction (John 10:10).

The Dawning of Time

In the beginning, God created the heavens and the earth (Genesis 1:1).

In the beginning, the earth was nothing like what we see today. It was shapeless, lifeless, and empty. Imagine a world without land or light or living things. There was only a dark and barren ocean. The spirit of God hovered over this watery canvas, and where God is, there is life and purpose. He would create something incredible in this place, something altogether amazing. Something that only He could do. This creation would be a stunning display of His glory.

The appearance of light was part of God's plan for shaping this masterpiece. He simply spoke and this light appeared. In an instant, the darkness was exposed. He called the light "day," and the darkness He called "night."

Then He created a space between the waters of the earth and the waters of the heavens. He called this space "sky." Today it is also known as the atmosphere. The atmosphere contains oxygen and other gases. It is an important part of the water and weather cycles, and it acts as a filter for the radiation produced by the sun. Without the sky, life on earth would be impossible.

Next, God directed the flow of all that water to one location and dry land to appear everywhere else. He called the dry land "earth" and the waters "seas." With perfect skill and artistry, God was shaping the world.

Genesis 1:1–10

God created our world in an orderly way. On the first day, He made the earth and filled it with light – just by speaking! Then He separated the water on the ground from the water that is in the air. This became the second day. God then spoke and made the waters come together in the oceans and made the land rise up into hills and mountains. God looked over everything that was made and said that it was good.

Beauty and Purpose

After forming the sky, oceans, and land, God filled these spaces with life.

A wide variety of plants sprouted from the earth. Trees, herbs, and grasses in diverse shades of green dotted the landscape. These plants yielded seeds after their own kind. This was an amazing design feature that made sure the plants could reproduce themselves. Not only were the plants beautiful, they would provide a steady supply of food and oxygen for the creatures that would soon come. God was creating a habitat that would last.

Next, He made the sun, moon, and stars. People are drawn to the sky and can't help gazing at its vast beauty. It has practical purposes also. From the earliest times, people learned to measure their days by sunlight, and weeks and months by the changing moon. This knowledge helped them know when to plant and when to harvest their crops. Also, the stars form constellations that have served as guides for people traveling by land or by sea. They are like a sparkling map in the sky.

Genesis 1:11—19

After creating heaven and earth and filling them with light, God spoke again and began calling plants and seeds to life. Growing things began to rise up and thrive. Out of the rich soil came beautiful flowers, delicious plants for vegetables, fruit trees, and more. This wondrous evening and morning of creation became the third day. God then placed the sun, moon, and stars up in the sky. These would light the world and help us mark days and nights, months, special times, and the seasons. This was His fourth day of creating.

The heavens declare the glory of God, and the sky above proclaims his handiwork. Day to day pours out speech, and night to night reveals knowledge. There is no speech, nor are there words, whose voice is not heard. Their voice goes out through all the earth, and their words to the end of the world (Psalm 19:1—4).

The Animal Kingdom

Next, God created a variety of aquatic creatures, from tiny snails to great big whales. God also made every kind of flying animal and pelicans, puffins, pigeons, parrots, and oh so many more! Birds of many colors, shapes, and songs took flight. Then He filled the earth with every kind of insect, amphibian, reptile, and mammal.

It must have been something to hear the singing, snorting, splashing, barking, roaring, buzzing, clomping, and chomping sounds of this wild new ecosystem. It was the world's very first "nature preserve." These animals would drink the water and breathe the oxygen from the first days of creation. They would eat the plants that came after that. Then they would "fertilize" the ground to help the next generation of plants grow strong.

Water, land, oxygen, plants, and living creatures thrived together. The sea, sky, and land were brimming with life. It was a miraculous accomplishment.

Genesis 1:20–25

On the fifth day, God created the sea creatures and the birds, and filled the waters and the skies with their life. From the smallest plankton to the largest whales, the ocean was made full of everything good. These creatures of the water along with the birds of the air were blessed by God and were told to fill the whole earth with life. Then came the sixth day of creation, and God spoke again. This time His words formed the smallest insects and the largest land animals. All the creeping, crawling kinds of the land found plenty of plants ready for them to eat.

Made in His Image

God saved His greatest creation for last. He made man in His own image. It can be hard to understand what that means since we have never seen God, but here are a few things to consider.

Human beings can think and act in ways that animals cannot. We feel emotions. We have imaginations and creative abilities. We can communicate thoughts and feelings and ask questions. We have the capacity for wisdom. We have the ability to discern right from wrong. These abilities were not given to animals but are a reflection of God's image in mankind.

Though we have a natural body, being created in the image of God means we also have a spiritual nature. It is with our spirit that we can "connect" with God through prayer. It is with our spirit that we come to understand spiritual things, and it is with our spirit that we can come to love and trust our Creator. No, we cannot know everything about God, but we can know enough to change our hearts and enrich our lives.

Adam was created first. His physical body was formed, and then God fashioned Eve from one of Adam's ribs. He chose to make her in this unique way to represent the unique bond shared by the man and the woman. They were one flesh, equal in value, and joined by God's design and blessing to perfectly complement one another. They were naked before their Creator, just like the animals. Yet they were not embarrassed or ashamed.

And God blessed them. And God said to them, "Be fruitful and multiply and fill the earth and subdue it, and have dominion over the fish of the sea and over the birds of the heavens and over every living thing that moves on the earth" (Genesis 1:28).

In other words, God gave them authority over His creation, charging them to take good care of it. Their job was to reflect God's glory and goodness everywhere they went and to teach their children to do the same.

It was a very good plan.

➳ *Genesis 1:26–31, 2*

Everything on earth had been created by God's spoken word. Well, everything had been created except people. While it was still the sixth day of creation, God formed the first person, a man called Adam. He took the dust and shaped it into a man and breathed life into him. Adam was made in the image of God. Then God formed Eve from one of Adam's ribs. God blessed Adam and Eve and told them to have children and to rule over the earth and its creatures.

Between Two Trees

The LORD planted a garden in the east of Eden. It was the most beautiful place on earth, a sanctuary filled with an abundance of beautiful plants and trees. Interesting animals were everywhere. Adam and Eve were in the Garden, and God met with them there.

A river flowed through Eden, providing water for every living thing. From there it divided into four branches that watered the land outside the sanctuary, making life possible there too. One day Adam and Eve would leave the Garden, but for now, the Garden was home. They were safe there in the loving presence of their Creator. They were healthy, happy, and free.

Now, there were two unique trees in the center of the Garden, the only ones of their kind. They were called the tree of life and the tree of the knowledge of good and evil. God told Adam he could eat the fruit of any tree in the Garden except the tree of the knowledge of good and evil. That fruit was forbidden. God told him that if he ate of it, he would die. At this point in time, nothing had ever died. Not a plant. Not an animal. Nothing.

If they ate of that tree, everything would change, and not for the better.

God wanted His children to love and trust Him, but He did not force them to. Genuine love and trust must be freely given. Adam and Eve were not prisoners or puppets. They had the freedom to choose for themselves how to live.

Genesis 2:8–16

When the seventh day came, God rested from all His creative work. It was after this that He planted a garden in an area called Eden. There was a river for fresh water flowing through the Garden, and it was filled with fruit trees and everything good that Adam and Eve would need to live there. Here they would take care of the Garden, and here they would live in perfect peace. There was no suffering and no sorrow, only joy. However, there was one tree in the garden that they were not supposed to eat from. This was called the tree of the knowledge of good and evil.

Hiding from God

Hiding from God

There was another presence in the garden. Disguised as a serpent, Satan spoke to Eve. Slyly, smoothly, he would try to convince her to eat the fruit God had forbidden. He knew it would cause sadness, pain, and even death one day, but Satan cared nothing for her.

He was very clever. First, he pretended to be something he was not. A simple serpent. A creature that Eve would have had no reason to fear at that time. Remember, nothing bad had ever happened. No one had ever been harmed by a serpent.

Next, he planted a seed of doubt in her mind. He said, "Did God actually say, 'You can't eat from any tree in the garden'?"

Satan wanted Eve to focus on the one thing God had forbidden instead of all the good things He had given her. If he could get her to do that, there was a good chance she would start to doubt God's word. But Eve knew what God had said. She told the serpent that if they ate of that tree they would die.

"You will not die, for God knows that when you eat it your eyes will be opened! You will be like God, knowing good and evil," Satan said. Why shouldn't she know both good and evil? Shouldn't she decide for herself what was right and what was wrong for her?

Eve had a choice — either trust the word of her Creator or the word of this clever creature. Remember, Adam and Eve had been told to rule over God's creation. She had the authority to send the serpent away. Sadly, that is not what happened. She took a bite of the fruit. At first it tasted good, so she gave some to Adam. Adam had heard God's warning, but he chose to eat the fruit also. With the first taste, the knowledge of good and evil entered their bodies. Sin became a part of them.

At that moment their eyes were opened, and they experienced guilt and shame for the first time. Their sin was now exposed. They sewed fig leaves together for clothing, but this paper-thin attempt to cover their guilt was useless. So, when God came looking for them, they hid among the trees.

Now, God already knew what they had done and where they were hiding. He knew they were afraid. There would be consequences for their decision, but they needed to know they could still come to Him. God called out for Adam, saying, "Where are you?"

Adam replied, "I heard you in the garden and I hid. I was afraid because I was naked." Then Adam and Eve confessed what they had done, but their confession was laced with blame for another. Adam blamed Eve, and Eve blamed the serpent.

Genesis 3:1–13

In the Garden of Eden with Adam and Eve was a serpent. This was no ordinary snake, but the evil one called Satan in the form of a snake. Satan came to trick Adam and Eve to see if he could get them to betray God. First, He spoke with Eve, asking her about the forbidden tree. Then the snake lied and said that what God said wasn't true. Surely, they wouldn't die if they ate from the tree of the knowledge of good and evil. So, Eve ate of the fruit then gave some to Adam, who also ate it. Soon all they felt was shame in this first sin.

The Aftermath

God's response was both just and merciful. The serpent had wanted to be exalted above God, so God cursed him to spend the rest of his life slinking along the ground, and his eventual destruction was foretold. A Savior would come one day who would crush his evil head.

After Adam and Eve chose to disobey God, they felt guilt for the first time. When He found them, they were hiding in the Garden. Because of his deception, the serpent was cursed by God to crawl on his belly. Because of her part, Eve would have pain whenever she gave birth to a child. Adam would be punished by having to work hard to harvest their food from the ground. Then both Adam and Eve were told to leave the beauty and peace of the Garden of Eden. They lost everything because of their sin that brought suffering to the whole world.

So the LORD God said to the serpent, "Because you have done this, 'Cursed are you above all livestock and all wild animals! You will crawl on your belly and you will eat dust all the days of your life. And I will put enmity between you and the woman, and between your offspring and hers; he will crush your head, and you will strike his heel" (Genesis 3:14–15; NIV).

God told Eve that she would experience pain in childbirth. This pain would be a reminder that disobeying God has unpleasant consequences.

God told Adam that the ground would now be cursed because he had chosen to listen to his wife instead of God. From that point on, Adam would struggle to make a living from the earth.

Adam and Eve had enjoyed a relationship of harmony and mutual respect. Going forward, there would be times of conflict in their marriage. Their perfect partnership had become a casualty of sin. Finally, they would have to leave Eden. God did not want people to live forever with a sinful nature, and that is what would have happened if they had also eaten of the tree of life.

Adam and Eve would eventually die as a result of living in a cursed world, but first they would have an opportunity to live and to see many generations of their family live outside the Garden. While they might still desire to reflect God's goodness and righteousness going forward, it would be much harder to do. Sin had become a part of them. They would fight temptation daily, and so would everyone who lived after them.

This may sound like a hopeless situation, but it was not. Even though Adam and Eve had broken their perfect relationship with God, He did not abandon them. Fig leaves did not provide adequate protection for Adam and Eve, so God made them sturdy clothing out of animal skins. This was the first time in history that blood was shed. Animals had to die so that the sin of man could be covered. How difficult it must have been for God to take the life of these beautiful animals He had recently created. He offered the very first sacrifice, and because of His great love, it would not be His last.

Genesis 3

Life on the Outside

So Adam and Eve were sent out of the Garden, and they headed into a wild and cursed landscape. It was an unknown land with unknown dangers. The first son born to them was named Cain. He grew up to be a farmer and raised crops from the ground. They had another son and named him Abel. He became a shepherd.

One year, when it was time for the harvest, Cain and Abel both offered a sacrifice to God. Cain chose to offer some of his crops as a gift to the LORD, but Abel offered the most perfect firstborn lamb from his herd.

God saw into their hearts and understood the motivation behind their gifts. He was pleased with Abel's sacrifice — it was like the one He Himself had made for Adam and Eve. He knew how hard it was for Abel to give up his little lamb. On the other hand, God was not satisfied with Cain's offering. This made Cain very angry. God told him he would be accepted if he did the right thing and warned him to take control of his emotions.

Cain did not listen to God. Instead, he let his anger and jealousy grow to the point that he did something terrible. He convinced Abel to walk with him out to a field, and there, Cain killed him.

God gave Cain a chance to own up to what he had done. He asked him, "Where is your brother Abel?" Cain would not confess or repent. Instead, he told God he didn't know where Abel was.

In time, after they left the Garden, Adam and Eve became the parents of two boys. Their oldest, Cain, grew up to be a farmer, and the younger son, Abel, grew up to be a shepherd. They both brought a sacrifice to the Lord. Cain brought something he had grown, and Abel brought an animal from his flock. Looking at their hearts, God accepted Abel's offering but not Cain's. This made Cain angry and jealous. In his anger, he killed his own brother and then lied to God about it. Even then, God showed mercy to Cain.

God replied, "What did you do? The voice of your brother's blood is crying out to me from the ground. So now you will be cursed from the ground and it will no longer produce crops for you."

What God had seen in Cain's heart was proved true by Cain's actions. He killed his brother out of jealousy. He had no remorse for what he had done and argued with God about his punishment. Ironically, he feared suffering the same fate he had inflicted on his brother. Even though Cain had shown no mercy to Abel, God showed mercy to Cain by putting a mark of protection on him so that he would not be killed. He would have time to consider his ways.

Then Cain fled to a faraway land. Away from Eden, away from his family, and away from the presence of God.

Genesis 4

Two Paths

Cain's story is a sad reminder of how one sin can lead to another. His pride led to jealousy. His jealousy led to uncontrolled anger, which led to him killing his brother. Finally, he lied. At any point along the way, Cain could have repented and stopped this sad series of events, but he did not. He would rather walk away from all he had known than admit his own guilt. The roots of sin run deep.

He eventually settled in a land to the east of Eden. He built a city and had many children and grandchildren. His descendants were builders, musicians, and craftsmen who went on to build even more cities. Cain's influence was spreading in that part of the world, but sadly, it was an influence that did not include God. He led his family to pursue fame, prosperity, and personal pleasure instead. Not surprisingly, with each new generation, sin and evil grew and prospered.

Cain had made his choice. He would not submit to the will and rule of God. So it is no surprise that he and his descendants were not spreading the good image of God anywhere. Instead, they were spreading selfishness, pride, anger, and violence.

Adam and Eve must have felt a great deal of regret as they experienced the painful consequences of their sin. One son was dead, and the other was lost to them. However, Eve conceived again and gave birth to another son.

This is the book of the generations of Adam. When God created man, he made him in the likeness of God. Male and female he created them, and he blessed them and named them Man when they were created. When Adam had lived 130 years, he fathered a son in his own likeness, after his image, and named him Seth. The days of Adam after he fathered Seth were 800 years; and he had other sons and daughters (Genesis 5:1–4).

When Seth was born, Eve said, "God has granted me another child in place of Abel." With this child came hope for a new beginning.

Seth's family would worship God. After his son Enosh was born, people first began to call on the name of the LORD. It would be through the line of Seth that God would fulfill the promise He had made in the Garden. One day, long in the future, a descendant of Seth would crush the head of the enemy, defeating Satan once and for all.

Adam and Eve lived for many more years and had many more children. God allowed them to see many generations of grandchildren before they died. He blessed them even as they lived in a world broken by their sin.

Cain and Seth offer examples of two very different ways to live. One led his family away from God, and the other led his family toward God. *Genesis 4–5*   *1 John 3:11–12*

Cain and Abel chose different pathways. The one path led Abel closer to God, while Cain walked away from God and His ways. Soon Cain's family followed his rebellious heart. His parents, Adam and Eve, eventually had a new child they named Seth. Seth grew up showing respect for God and His ways, just as Abel had. It was through the family of Seth that the promised Savior would come. All people have the same choice to make as Cain and Abel and Seth did.

Thread of Hope

God is the giver and sustainer of life. He is holy and altogether different than humans.

Mankind was created in the image of God, who is perfectly righteous. Until they sinned, Adam and Eve were righteous also. This gave them the right to live forever in God's holy presence. Adam and Eve chose another path. Satan entered the Garden and tempted Eve to disobey God. She listened to him and ate the fruit. Then she invited her husband to eat it also, and he did.

Because they sinned, Adam and Eve would have to leave the Garden and God's life-sustaining presence. They would have to live in a world that was cursed, and they would eventually die a natural death. God had a plan to spare them from eternal death. He had promised in the Garden that one day Eve's offspring would crush the head of the enemy. That promise would be fulfilled in Jesus Christ, but until He came, God would mercifully allow the sacrificial death of animals to stand in the place of humans. One life for another, their scarlet blood pointing to the perfect sacrifice that was yet to come.

Even in a cursed world, Adam and Eve could still know God. They could choose to love and obey Him. Sadly, they could also know evil and could choose to love and obey it as well. They would be faced with that choice for the rest of their lives, and so would everyone who lived after them. Cain and Seth serve as examples of these two choices.

- People who follow the path of Cain will insist on deciding for themselves what is right and what is wrong. They will not respect what God says about a matter. Instead, they will follow their own thoughts, feelings, and desires that have been distorted by sin. They will seek the honor and glory of mankind. This path leads to everlasting death (Proverbs 14:12).

- People who follow the path of Seth will desire to live in a way that honors God. They will accept that He is the supreme being who knows what is best. They will accept His instruction along with His love and His blessing. They will love Him in return and seek His honor and glory instead of man's. Even so, they will still fall short at times. On this path, God provides atonement for sin. This path leads to everlasting life (John 3:16).

glo·ry	of great honor, fame, or importance
ho·ly	perfectly good, pure, set apart from that which is not perfectly good or pure
of·fer·ing	a gift or donation
a·tone	to make up for, or to make something right again

A Flood Is Coming!

A Flood Is Coming!

There were likely millions of people living on the earth by the time Noah came along. It had been over 1,000 years since Adam and Eve had left the Garden. Sadly, by this time, the hearts of almost everyone alive had turned cold toward God. More people had chosen the path of Cain than the path of Noah's ancestor Seth. Sin and wickedness prevailed on the earth. Satan must have been pleased.

Having seen enough, God was about to intervene in history. Noah was not a perfect man, but he walked with the LORD. He was a man of integrity and a preacher of righteousness. God told Noah He was going to send a Flood to clear the earth of corruption. Water would cover even the tallest mountains. It would wash away all evidence of man's rebellion.

God told Noah to build a large boat (or ark). The Ark would shelter Noah's family and a selection of animals during the Flood. This project took many years to complete, but Noah trusted God and did everything He said. When the time came, Noah and his wife, along with their three sons and their wives, entered the Ark. Then God closed the door, shutting them safely inside. There were eight people on board, along with male and female pairs of the animal kinds.

Then water burst forth from underground springs, and rain fell from the sky. It was a hard rain that did not stop for 40 days and nights. By this time, the earth was blanketed in water, just as it had been on the first day of creation. Every living thing on the land perished.

Noah and his family spent the next several months at sea. They were safe and had everything they needed. No doubt, they were very thankful to be alive. Finally, the water began to recede. They must have been overjoyed when they began to see mountaintops peeking out of the water.

Genesis 6–7, 8:1-5

2 Peter 2:5

Over one thousand years had passed since Adam and Eve left Eden. Millions of people lived in the world, but few remained who loved God. However, God saw Noah, one who stayed true to Him. God told Noah that a Flood was coming to cover the whole world. These waters were coming because of all the evil. Noah and his family would need to build an Ark, a large boat, for them and the creatures of the earth. When they finished, a rain began to fall. Noah, his family, and the animal pairs were carried safely on the Ark.

A Fresh Start

Eventually the Ark came to rest on the mountains of Ararat. Noah watched and waited. He waited for the landscape to appear. He waited for the ground to dry out. He waited for trees and plants to sprout and grow. Mostly, he waited for God's instruction. When the time was right, God told Noah to leave the Ark.

It must have been wonderful to walk on dry land again, and to find fertile ground for crops and space for their family to grow. Imagine watching the animals scamper, run, and climb as they explored their new environment. What a joyful sound they must have made! Hope for a fresh start was all around.

The first thing Noah did was build an altar and prepare a sacrifice of thanksgiving to the LORD, for He had saved them from the Flood. Then God blessed Noah and his sons. Just as He had instructed Adam and Eve so many years ago, He told them to be fruitful and multiply. He gave them a new chance to carry His good image to the ends of the earth.

God told Noah that so long as the earth remained, there would be planting and harvest, cold and heat, summer and winter, and day and night. He would never send another flood to wash away man's wickedness. Instead, He gave Noah instructions for dealing with man's sinful nature. For the time being, people would be responsible for conducting their own justice.

Then God placed a rainbow in the clouds. It was a sign of His promise to never again destroy the earth with water. Still today, rainbows serve to remind God's people of His power, His protection, and His promise.

Genesis 8—9

After the heavy rains stopped and the water began drying up, the Ark of Noah found a resting place on the mountains of Ararat. When he and his family could finally step outside, they offered a sacrifice to God. This was to give thanks to God for saving them and the creatures of the world. God made a promise that the earth would never be flooded like this again. This promise was marked by a rainbow in the clouds. Rainbows are reminders of God's promise still today.

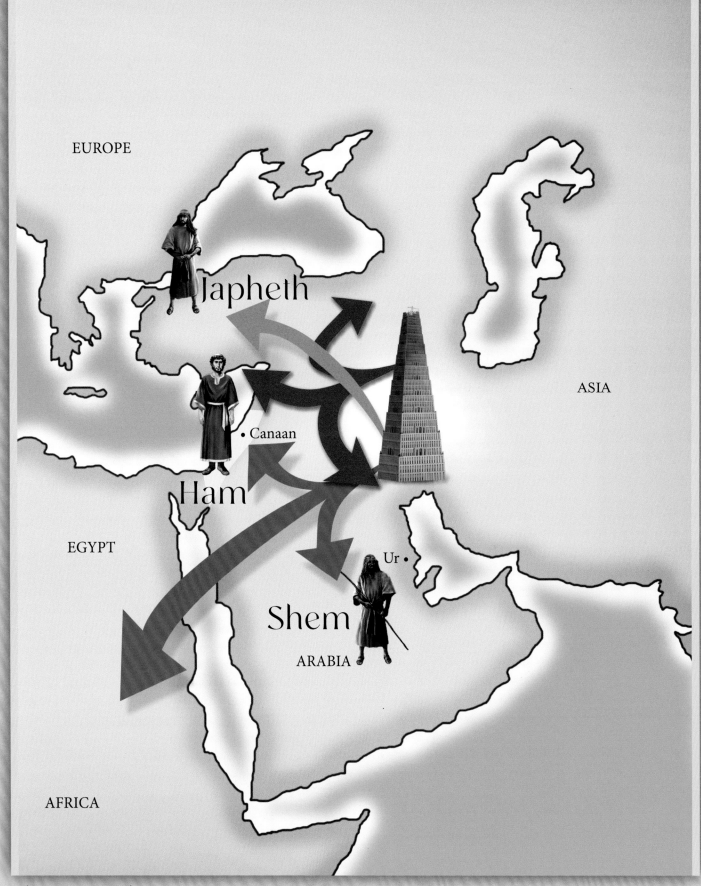

EUROPE

ASIA

Japheth

Canaan

Ham

EGYPT

Ur •

Shem

ARABIA

AFRICA

Pride Meets Providence

God had told Noah and his family to migrate over the earth. However, Noah's sons and their families found a pleasant plain in the land of Shinar (also known as Babylonia) and decided to settle there instead. They did not want to separate and move to unknown lands. They wanted to stay together. They wanted to decide for themselves where to live.

So they built a city and began construction on a tall tower. This ancient skyscraper was the first of its kind. It was a monument to their prideful rebellion. They said, "Let's build a city, with a tower that reaches to the heavens. We will make a great name for ourselves here instead of spreading out over the earth."

It had not taken long for Noah's family to repeat the sins of their ancestors. The LORD knew that the intent of their hearts was evil. They had to be stopped or soon the world would be full of wickedness again.

At this time, all of Noah's descendants spoke the same language. This made it easy for them to stick together. So God confused their tongues. Suddenly, different families began speaking different languages. Imagine their confusion and frustration as they tried to understand one another. It became hard to get along and impossible to work together. Their big city dream was finished. This city came to be known as "Babel," which means confusion.

The families of Shem, Ham, and Japheth spread out in every direction according to their new languages. As they walked away from Babel, confusion went with them. They would go on to settle various parts of the earth. They would build other cities and civilizations. At the same time, they created new and various false "gods" that were more to their liking — gods they believed they could control. The worship of these false gods often required evil acts and sacrifices that were inspired by Satan, the great deceiver.

This is how the different nations of the world began. God saw to it that His plan to populate the whole earth would be followed one way or another, while the plans of men came to nothing.

Genesis 11

Noah and his family were supposed to fill the earth with their families and their faith. However, when they found land that seemed pleasing, they stopped traveling. After many years, Noah's descendants decided to build a tower to the sky to bring fame to themselves, but God saw their hearts and knew this tower would only increase their pride. Because they all spoke one language, He mixed up their languages so they would only be able to speak to a small group of people. Soon everyone went out from this city now known as Babel to fill the whole earth with people as God intended.

Out of a Far Country

Ten generations later, Terah (a descendant of Shem) lived in Mesopotamia with his three sons — Abram, Nahor, and Haran. They lived in Ur, a prosperous city near the Euphrates River. There were nice homes, gardens, markets, libraries, schools, and temples in Ur. The people who migrated here had created a fine city to live in, but they worshiped false gods.

God wanted mankind to understand that the idols they worshiped were not really gods at all. He is the one true God, and He wanted people to know it. So He set out to create a nation of people who would do just that. This nation would begin with Terah's son Abram.

One day, God spoke to Abram. Abram had surely heard stories of a God who had spoken to his ancestor Noah. So when he heard this voice for himself, he paid attention.

"Go from your country and your kindred and your father's house to the land that I will show you. And I will make of you a great nation, and I will bless you and make your name great, so that you will be a blessing. I will bless those who bless you, and him who dishonors you I will curse, and in you all the families of the earth shall be blessed" (Genesis 12:1–3).

Abram listened and obeyed. God led him to the land of Canaan, only to find that the descendants of Ham had previously settled the land and created their own false gods. God told Abram to settle there, so that is what he did.

One day, Abram asked the LORD how he would become a great nation since he and his wife, Sarai, had been unable to have children. Then the LORD told Abram to look at the night sky and said, "Look up at the sky and count the stars — if you can even count them. That's how many descendants you will have."

Abram believed the LORD, and that pleased the LORD. God entered into a covenant with him and gave him a new name, Abraham, which means "father of many nations." He also gave Abraham's wife, Sarai, the new name Sarah because she would be the mother of nations. Together, they would form a new nation of people, and the LORD would be their God.

Then God told Abraham that his descendants would be slaves in another land for 400 years. After that, they would inherit the land of Canaan. So Abraham knew that the fulfillment of God's promise would be a long time coming. Faith does not always produce an immediate reward.

Many years after Babel, and many miles from there in a land called Ur, God spoke to a man named Abram. God called Abram to leave his home and family to follow God's plan. God wanted to make Abram, his wife, Sarai, and their descendants into a nation that would bless the whole world. Though Abram and his wife were old and had no children, God promised them a child. God changed the man's name to Abraham, which means "father of many nations." His wife's name was changed to Sarah. Their faith would be mentioned throughout Scripture.

Genesis 12, 15, 17

Joshua 24:2

Son of the Promise

After many years, Sarah gave up on having a child and suggested that Abraham have a baby with her servant, Hagar. Neither she nor Abraham asked God about this idea, but Abraham agreed. So he and Hagar had a son together and named him Ishmael. Naturally, there was tension in this home. God had intended marriage to be between one man and one woman, not two. Sarah became jealous of Hagar.

God had not needed Abraham and Sarah to help Him fulfill His promise. He had told them that a new nation would come from their union, and He was faithful to that promise. Miraculously, when Abraham was 100 years old and Sarah was in her nineties, they had a son and named him Isaac.

Once Sarah had her own child, she insisted that Abraham send Hagar and Ishmael away. Abraham was sad to see Ishmael go. God comforted him, saying, "Do not be sad about the boy. Isaac will carry on the family name, but I will make Ishmael into a nation also." Ishmael had been born because Abraham and Sarah had not trusted God. Nevertheless, God loved and blessed Ishmael. He became a skilled archer and eventually settled in the desert of Paran, far away from his father. He went on to have 12 sons and a daughter, and in time, they did indeed become a large nation.

One day, God decided to test Abraham's faith. He told him to take young Isaac to the top of a mountain and sacrifice him there.

Abraham must have been confused, but he did what God said anyway. He placed his beloved son on an altar. Then God called out to him, "Abraham! Do not hurt the boy. Now I see that you truly trust me because you were willing to give your son up for me." Just then, Abraham saw a ram that was caught in a brier nearby. He took the animal and offered it as a sacrifice in the place of his son. Then God said to him, "Because you have honored me, I will bless your descendants. In your offspring shall all the nations of the earth be blessed."

Genesis 16–17, 21–22, 26

John 3:16

Abraham and Sarah waited for the time they would have a baby, but she seemed unable to have a child. She thought Abraham should have this child of promise through her servant, Hagar. When Abraham and Hagar's boy was born, they named him Ishmael. Then as God had promised, Abraham and Sarah had a son together in their old age. They named him Isaac. Sarah became jealous of Hagar, so they decided to send her and Ishmael away into the desert. Then God asked Abraham to sacrifice his beloved son, Isaac. He was going to do this to honor God, but God provided a ram for the sacrifice instead.

A Family for Isaac

A Family for Isaac

Years later, the time came for Isaac to marry, but Abraham did not want his son to marry a local woman. He was afraid they would persuade him to worship the false gods of the land. So he sent a trusted servant, Eliezer, back to the land he had come from. Abraham's brother Nahor still lived there, so Abraham told Eliezer to find Isaac a wife from his brother's family.

When Eliezer got there, he went to the local well and prayed. He asked the LORD to help him find the right wife for Isaac. "May it be that when I say to a young woman, 'Please give me a drink,' and she says, 'Drink, and I'll water your camels too' — then I will know she is the one you have chosen."

Before he had even finished praying, a young woman named Rebekah arrived at the well. She did exactly as Eliezer had asked. Then she told him she was the granddaughter of Nahor. Eliezer was so thankful! He bowed down and worshiped the LORD for answering his prayer.

Rebekah agreed to marry Isaac, and she left for Canaan with Eliezer. Isaac and Rebekah were childless for the first 20 years of their marriage. Then God blessed them with twins. One day, God told Rebekah, "Two nations are in your womb; one will be stronger than the other, and the older will serve the younger."

Esau was born first, making him the oldest. Jacob was born shortly after, with his hand grabbing Esau's heel. Though they were twins, they looked nothing alike, and they had very different personalities. Esau loved to be outdoors. He grew up to be a skillful hunter who enjoyed bringing home wild game, making him the favorite son of Isaac. Jacob preferred to stay near home and was favored by his mother.

Genesis 24, 25:19–28

Isaac grew up strong in the Lord. When it was time for him to marry, his father Abraham sent a trusted servant, Eliezer, back to their homeland to find him a wife. Eliezer traveled there and prayed that God would lead him to the right woman. As he finished praying, the Lord led Rebekah to him. She showed kindness to Eliezer and told him she was of the household of Nahor. This was the sign Eliezer needed, and soon Rebekah was journeying back with him to Isaac. In time, she had twin sons named Jacob and Esau. God said they would become two nations.

Of Birthrights and Blessings

In those days, the firstborn son became the head of the family after his father died. This was known as the birthright. Isaac had received the birthright from Abraham and would pass it on to his firstborn son also. God told Isaac,

"Sojourn in this land, and I will be with you and will bless you, for to you and to your offspring I will give all these lands, and I will establish the oath that I swore to Abraham your father. I will multiply your offspring as the stars of heaven and will give to your offspring all these lands. And in your offspring all the nations of the earth shall be blessed, because Abraham obeyed my voice and kept my charge, my commandments, my statutes, and my laws" (Genesis 26:3–5).

Everyone assumed that Esau would inherit the birthright when Isaac died, but Esau did not take this responsibility seriously. First, he had married two Canaanite women against his parents' wishes. Then he had sold his birthright to his younger brother. It happened as he returned from hunting one day. He was very hungry and found his brother had made a pot of stew. Esau asked for some. Jacob told him he would only give it to him in exchange for his birthright. Esau agreed to this, selling his place as head of the family for a bowl of stew. Esau showed disrespect for his parents, his position, and for the LORD with these decisions. Jacob took advantage of his brother's impulsive nature and secured the birthright for himself.

During this time in history, the firstborn son would become the head of the household when the father died. As Esau was the firstborn, it was expected that he would get this birthright. Yet, that is not what happened. Esau sold his birthright to his brother, Jacob, for a pot of stew. Esau also married two women from Canaan against the wishes of his parents. His poor decisions cost him the birthright.

Now, it was also the custom in those days for the father to declare a blessing over his children before he died. The firstborn son usually received a special blessing. Even though Esau had sold his birthright, Isaac planned to give him the firstborn blessing anyway. One day, Isaac sent Esau out to get some wild game, saying that he would bless him after eating it.

Genesis 25:29–34, 26:34–35, 27

Hebrews 12:15–16

Rebekah's Plan

Rebekah believed Jacob should receive the blessing instead of Esau because God had told her long ago that the older son would serve the younger. We are left to wonder if she had ever shared God's words with her husband. Regardless, Isaac and Rebekah disagreed on this important issue. So, while Esau was out hunting, Rebekah devised a plan to trick her husband.

Isaac was nearly blind in his old age, so she told Jacob to dress in Esau's clothes and pretend to be his brother. Jacob agreed. He even wrapped some goat skin around his arms so that he would appear to be hairy like Esau. Then he took some meat to his father and waited for the blessing.

At first Isaac was suspicious. Was this really his son Esau? But eventually, he was convinced, and he gave his blessing. "May God give to you the dew of heaven and the richness of the earth — an abundance of grain and new wine. May people serve you and nations bow down to you. May you be the master of your brothers. May those who curse you be cursed, and those who bless you be blessed." The plan had worked.

Rebekah and Jacob's deception was uncovered when Esau returned from hunting. Isaac was angry — to the point of trembling, but custom did not permit him to take the blessing back. He told Esau, "Look, I have made Jacob your master, I have given him servants, and I have sustained him with grain and new wine. What is left that I can do for you, my son?"

Esau cried out, "Do you have only one blessing, my father? Please bless me too!" Then Isaac said, "Behold, your dwelling place shall be away from the richness of the land, away from the dew of heaven above. You shall live by the sword and serve your brother. Yet the time will come when you will tear his yoke from your neck."

Esau was bitter. Not only had Jacob taken his birthright, now he had taken his blessing as well. So he plotted to kill his brother. Rebekah heard about Esau's plan, so she convinced Isaac to send Jacob away.

"It is time for Jacob to get married," she said, knowing that her husband would send him back to Paddan Aram (Haran) to find a wife from her brother's family. Rebekah believed that with time, Esau would forget what had happened and Jacob could come home.

Genesis 25, 27—28

Along with the family birthright, the firstborn son would often receive a special blessing from his father as well. Rebekah, Jacob's mother, thought he deserved this over his brother, Esau. She made a plan to trick her own husband, who had grown frail and blind. While Esau was away hunting, she helped disguise Jacob as Esau and brought him to Isaac. The trick worked, and Jacob received the special blessing. When Esau came back, he became angry and bitter. There was no taking back the blessing. Now Esau wanted to kill his brother, but God had another plan.

The Bride Price

So Isaac sent Jacob to Paddan Aram, saying, "Go at once and find a wife from among the daughters of your uncle Laban. May God Almighty bless you and make you fruitful and increase your numbers until you become a community of peoples. May he give you and your descendants the blessing given to Abraham."

Jacob quickly left Canaan, taking only a walking stick. He headed toward his mother's family, but no doubt this was a difficult journey. He was running from the only home he had ever known, and he was alone, giving him plenty of time to think about what he had done.

One night, Jacob had a dream. In this dream he saw a ladder that stretched from heaven to earth, with angels going up and down the ladder. God spoke to Jacob in that dream. He told him that He would bless him and his descendants. In fact, all the peoples of the earth would be blessed through him. The message was clear. Even though Jacob had done wrong, God's plan would not fail.

Jacob arrived at Paddan Aram and went to the local well where he met his cousin Rachel. Then his uncle Laban invited him to come and stay with them. The journey from Canaan had been a long and lonely one. How good it must have been to be among family again. It did not take long for Jacob to fall in love with Rachel. He told Laban he would tend his flocks for seven years if he could marry her. Laban agreed, and the years passed quickly for Jacob. When the time came, the wedding plans were made, and Jacob was looking forward to his marriage. He had no idea that Laban was about to trick him.

You see, Rachel had an older sister named Leah, and it was not customary to let the younger sister get married before the older. So, Laban replaced Rachel with Leah in the wedding ceremony. It was dark when the wedding feast ended, and Leah wore a veil that covered her face, so Jacob thought he was marrying the woman he loved. It was not until the next morning that he realized what had happened.

Of course, Jacob was angry. So, Laban promised Jacob he could also marry Rachel in one week's time, if he agreed to work another seven years for him. Laban was a shrewd man. His flocks had flourished under Jacob's care. He figured out a way to get both of his daughters married and keep Jacob around for another seven years. Jacob loved Rachel, so he agreed, and one week later, they were married.

Genesis 28, 29:1–28, 32:10

Jacob and his mother had tricked his father into giving a special blessing that was meant for his brother, Esau. This had made Esau angry, and he wanted to kill Jacob. So, Isaac sent Jacob back to their homeland to find someone to marry. On his journey, Jacob had a dream of angels going up and down a ladder between earth and heaven. God spoke to Jacob in the dream that He would bless him, his family, and all the peoples of the earth through him. Jacob fell in love with Rachel and married her, but not before he was tricked into also marrying Rachel's older sister, Leah. Jacob agreed to work for Laban for seven years for each of his wives.

Thread of Hope

God offered mankind another new beginning through the family of Noah. The first thing Noah did upon leaving the Ark was to offer an animal as a sacrifice to God. There were precious few animals left after the Flood, so it must have been especially hard to lose one. Thankfully, God had told Noah to take along extra of the clean animals for this very purpose (Genesis 7:23).

Noah lived for 350 years after the Flood. He surely tried to influence his family to follow the Lord, but at some point, they rebelled. They wanted to do as they pleased. They followed the path of Cain. No doubt Satan had fueled that desire in them, and they allowed it to take hold and flourish. So, God confused and divided this rebellious lot for their own good.

Many years later, God revealed Himself to Abram, a man who had been raised with many idols and false gods. He called Abram out of idolatry. There is so much hope in this story. Even when it looked like the whole world was following the wrong path, God was at work, making Himself known. Neither the works of Satan nor the foolishness of man would stop Him.

He entered into a covenant with Abram and gave him a new name. He and Sarah would start a family that would become a new nation, a special people. God would give them a land of their own and another chance to bear the good image of God. Abraham's new name was a symbol of his leaving idolatry and placing his faith in the one true God.

Abraham was not a perfect man. He and Sarah took matters into their own hands when they chose to have a child with Hagar, but he learned from his mistake. Going forward, he chose to believe and obey God even when he didn't understand — and even to the point that he was willing to offer his own beloved son to God.

Here we see again the beautiful scarlet thread. God provided a ram to take Isaac's place. He spared Abraham and Isaac from the heartache of death that day. Though the time would come when God would not spare His own heart. Or His own Son. Instead, He would offer His Son as a sacrifice for all of mankind. Such is the love of God.

We can learn a lot from Abraham's example. He listened when he heard God's voice. Then he chose to trust that voice. He left his home, his idols, and much of his family behind to follow God to an unknown land. Though he wasn't perfect, he desired to honor God with his life and decisions. Abraham's faith was evident in his actions.

Both of Abraham's sons would become great nations, just as God said. Though it would be through the line of Isaac that His covenant promise would be fulfilled.

wor·ship	to regard as holy to give all respect and honor to
i·dol	something or someone that is worshiped, a statue or image of that which is worshiped
cov·e·nant	an agreement between two or more people

The Long Walk Home

*I*t is hard to imagine how difficult it must have been to live in Jacob's house. Jacob and Rachel were in love, but he also had an obligation to take care of Leah. Somehow, they were all supposed to live together.

Leah began to have children, but Rachel could not get pregnant. So, even though Jacob loved her more than Leah, Rachel was jealous of her older sister. In a desperate attempt to provide children to Jacob, she insisted he have children with her servant Bilhah.

Not to be outdone, Leah then told Jacob to have children with her servant Zilpah. It became a competition to see which sister could give Jacob the most children. Finally, after many years, Rachel was able to have a child of her own. She named him Joseph. In all, Jacob had 12 sons with four different women.

Jacob worked for Laban for 14 years and then prepared to move his family back to Canaan. Laban had become quite rich because of Jacob, so he tried to convince him to stay a while longer. He promised Jacob part of his flock as payment, but he secretly planned to cheat him again.

One day while Laban was away from home, the LORD told Jacob to go ahead and leave. Jacob packed up his family and his flock and snuck away. Jacob was in a difficult situation. He knew that Laban would be angry and come after them. He also knew he would have to face his brother, Esau, at some point down the road. He was caught in the middle with enemies on both sides.

Sure enough, Laban and his men overtook them in Gilead, but with the LORD's help, Jacob was able to make peace with him. As they traveled on toward Canaan, Jacob heard that his brother, Esau, was riding out to meet him, and Esau had 400 men with him. Jacob feared the worst. His brother was coming to kill him!

Jacob began working for his uncle Laban and trying to create a home of peace for his new wives. Leah began to have children, heirs for Jacob, but Rachel could not have children. In her jealousy, Rachel gave Jacob her servant, Bilhah, to hope for more children. Leah then gave her servant, Zilpah, to Jacob. After the others had all given Jacob children, his wife Rachel became pregnant. This son would be named Joseph and would become his favorite. Now Jacob could return home, but he would be met by hundreds of his brother's men coming to meet him.

Jacob divided his family into two camps in hopes that some of them would be able to escape. Then he cried out to the Lord, "O God of my father Abraham, God of my father Isaac, Lord, you told me to return home. I don't deserve all the kindness and faithfulness you have shown me. I had only a walking stick when I crossed this Jordan the first time, but now I have much. Please save me from Esau. I am afraid he will come and attack me and my family, but you have said, 'I will surely make you prosper and will make your descendants like the sand of the sea, which cannot be counted.' "

Genesis 29:31–35, 30–32

Jacob Wrestles with God

The next morning, Jacob selected "gifts" from his livestock to send ahead to his brother. Perhaps Esau would be kind to him if he gave him something of value. He sent his family on ahead toward Canaan. Jacob stayed behind. He was anxious and afraid and no doubt needed some time alone to pray.

That night, a strange man showed up, and Jacob ended up in a wrestling match with him. They wrestled through the night, but Jacob refused to give up. Even after his hip was injured in the fight, Jacob held on. The man tried to leave, but Jacob told him he would not let go unless the man blessed him. The man said, "From now on, your name will be Israel instead of Jacob. For you have struggled with men and with God and have overcome."

Jacob realized his struggle had been with God, and he was amazed that his life had been spared. God had given him a new name, just as he had done with Jacob's grandfather Abraham. Jacob now had the courage to go and meet his brother.

We don't know what was in Esau's heart when he first set out to meet Jacob. The fact that he had 400 men with him has led many to believe he was indeed planning to kill his brother, but when he finally saw Jacob, he ran and embraced him instead. The Bible does not tell us Esau's motives, but it does tell us that he took his family and moved away from Jacob after this encounter. The only other time they saw each other was when they buried their father.

Esau's descendants became known as the Edomites, who would be enemies of Jacob's descendants (Israel) for generations to come.

Isaac's words to both his sons did indeed come to pass.

» *Genesis 27:28–29, 32, 39–40*

» *Deuteronomy 2:12*

» *Amos 1:11–12*

As Jacob approached his home and his brother, Esau, he sent gifts ahead, hoping to soften his heart. Jacob also sent his family away while he waited behind to see what would happen. He wrestled with a man throughout the night. As morning approached, the man tried to get away, but Jacob stopped him. He wanted the man to bless him. The man said that Jacob would now be called Israel, which means "he wrestles with God." Then Jacob set out to meet his brother, who embraced him warmly.

The Favorite Son

Jacob eventually arrived in Canaan with his family and was reunited with his father, but it was a bittersweet homecoming. His beloved mother, Rebekah, had already died, and his wife Rachel had died in childbirth along the way.

Jacob and the rest of his family settled in Canaan. The sons of Leah were Reuben, Simeon, Levi, Judah, Issachar, and Zebulun. The sons of Rachel were Joseph and Benjamin. The sons of Bilhah were Dan and Naphtali, and the sons of Zilpah were Gad and Asher.

Now, Jacob loved Joseph more than any of his other sons. He even gave him an expensive, colorful robe. This robe was a constant reminder to his brothers that Joseph was the favorite. Naturally, they were jealous of him. After Joseph told them about some of his dreams, they began to hate him. His dreams suggested that one day he would be their ruler, and they would bow down to him.

One day, Jacob sent Joseph to check on his brothers who were tending the flocks. When they saw him coming, they talked of killing this "dreamer." "Let's not kill him. After all, he is our brother," Judah said. He convinced them to sell Joseph to a caravan of slave traders instead.

Then they dipped Joseph's robe in some goat's blood and took it to their father, hoping he would believe Joseph had been killed by a wild animal, which is exactly what happened. Jacob's heart was broken. Even though they tried, Joseph's brothers could not make him feel better.

Meanwhile, Joseph was taken to Egypt. He was sold to Potiphar, an important officer in Egypt's army, but the LORD was with him. When Potiphar realized that Joseph made wise decisions, he put him in charge of his entire household. So, even though he was a slave, Joseph had a pretty good life, at least until Potiphar's wife made a mess of things.

She tried to convince Joseph to join her in cheating on Potiphar. Joseph's refusal made her very angry, and she lied to her husband, saying that Joseph had attacked her. So Potiphar had Joseph thrown into prison.

Genesis 35, 37, 39

Jacob and his family now settled back with his father in Canaan. Jacob loved Joseph more than any of his other sons. Out of his deep love for him, Jacob gave Joseph a wondrous, colorful robe. This love made the other brothers jealous. When Joseph mentioned that he had dreams of his whole family bowing before him, the brothers became angry. Their first plan was simply to kill him, but they decided instead to sell him as a slave. Soon Joseph would find himself in prison because of lies spoken against him.

Joseph's Rise to Power

Joseph's dreams came from God. Even in prison, he found himself in charge of the other prisoners. Two former servants of the king were put in that prison too. Both of them had troubling dreams they couldn't understand. However, Joseph had a gift from God. With his gift, he could understand that the cupbearer of the king would soon get his job back and the baker would soon be put to death. All happened as Joseph had said. Within two years, he was standing before the king, who was also having troubling dreams. Using his gift from God, soon Joseph was made second in command of Egypt.

It did not take long for the head guard of the prison to notice that Joseph was smart and honest. Joseph was soon put in charge of the entire prison. Sometime later, the king of Egypt (also called Pharaoh) sent two of his officials to that same prison. One was the king's baker and the other his cupbearer. One morning, Joseph arrived to find both men upset. They'd had bad dreams the night before and did not understand their meaning.

Joseph was able to interpret their dreams with the LORD's help. The cupbearer's dream meant he would soon get out of prison, but the baker's dream meant he would soon be executed. Three days later, this is exactly what happened.

After the cupbearer was released, he forgot all about Joseph — until two years later when the king himself had some disturbing dreams. None of the wise men or magicians of Egypt could interpret them. That is when the cupbearer remembered Joseph. The king sent for Joseph, and he was able to interpret the dream. He explained that Egypt would have seven years of prosperity followed by seven years of famine. "You should hire a wise man to prepare ahead for the hard times to come," Joseph said.

The king realized that God was with Joseph, so he made him governor and placed him in charge of all of Egypt! Joseph went from prisoner to prefect (a leading official) in one day. No one in the country was more powerful, except the king himself. During his first seven years in office, Joseph collected and stored huge quantities of grain. There was so much grain that he eventually stopped keeping records because it was beyond measure.

Joseph married an Egyptian woman and had two sons. He named the first Manasseh, saying, "The LORD has made me forget my troubles and my father's household." The second son was named Ephraim, meaning, "God has made me fruitful in the land of my suffering."

We can learn a great deal from Joseph's life and example. He certainly could have grown bitter over his fate. Being kidnapped and thrown into prison was not fair. Yet, instead of feeling sorry for himself, he made the best of his situation, and trusted God in good times and bad.

Genesis 39:20–23, 40–41

Money for Grain

The famine came, just as Joseph had predicted. So he opened the storehouses and sold grain to the Egyptians and the surrounding nations. Then after the people's money ran out, he allowed them to trade their land for food. In this way Joseph was able to increase the king's territory and wealth.

Back in Canaan, Jacob and his family were hard hit by the famine. So he sent his older sons to Egypt to buy grain. When the men arrived in Egypt, they bowed down before the governor, having no idea he was their brother. (Joseph had changed a lot in the years since they had seen him.) Joseph recognized his brothers, but he chose not to tell them who he was. Instead, he decided to test them to see if they had changed.

First, he accused them of being spies, a crime that carried the death sentence. Then he had them thrown into prison, where he overheard them say they were being punished by God for what they had done to Joseph. Apparently, they did feel some remorse for what they had done to him. However, Joseph left them in prison awhile longer.

After three days, the brothers pleaded with the governor to let them take food back to their father and youngest brother, Benjamin. Joseph agreed to let them go but kept Simeon behind in the prison. He promised to release him if they returned with Benjamin. Then he sent them on their way.

Now, he had secretly told his servant to put the money they had used to buy grain back in their traveling bags. He knew that his brothers would be terrified when they found the money — they could be accused of stealing! Would they risk returning to free Simeon? Joseph would have to wait and see.

Genesis 42

One of the king's troubling dreams had been interpreted by Joseph to mean a famine would come to Egypt. After a seven-year period of abundance, this famine began. People from all over this part of the world came to Egypt to buy food. Even Joseph's brothers came, hoping to get some food if they could. Though Joseph recognized them, they did not know who he was, so he tested them. As second in command over Egypt, Joseph had them thrown in prison as spies. Then he let all but Simeon leave and told them to bring their youngest brother when they returned.

From Famine to Forgiveness

From Famine to Forgiveness

When Jacob's sons got home, they told their father what had happened. At first he refused to let Benjamin go back to Egypt, but he finally realized there was no other choice. His family was in danger of starving. So all of his sons left for Egypt, but this time they took double the money. They intended to give back what they had found in their sacks, as well as buy more grain.

When Joseph heard his brothers had arrived, he had them brought to his house. They were terrified that the governor would accuse them of stealing so they spoke to the man who had taken their money before. He remembered them and said, "Do not be afraid. I remember taking your money. Your God must have given you the money that was in your sacks."

Simeon was reunited with his brothers, and together, Jacob's 11 sons waited for the governor to arrive. When he arrived, they bowed down before him yet again. Joseph was pleased that his brothers had been honest about the money, and he was happy to see that Benjamin was with them. He invited them to stay for lunch, and to their amazement, he seated them in the order of their birth. These men who had been afraid just a short time before were now dining with the governor of Egypt. What a surprising turn of events!

Joseph had prepared one final test for them. He sent them on their way, but he had secretly placed his own silver cup in Benjamin's sack. Then he sent soldiers after them to accuse them of stealing it. When all was said and done, Benjamin had been found with the cup and would not be allowed to leave. The rest were free to go.

Judah pleaded with the governor, telling him about all the family had been through since their brother Joseph had "died." He told him it would break their father's heart if they did not bring Benjamin home. Finally, he offered to stay as a prisoner in his brother's place. Judah had certainly done some bad things, but he had once saved Joseph's life. Now he offered to stay in prison so that Benjamin could go free.

Finally, Joseph was satisfied. He was overcome with emotion and wept as he revealed his true identity to his brothers. "I am Joseph, your brother, the one you sold into Egypt! Don't be afraid or angry with yourselves that you sold me into this place, because it was to save lives that God sent me before you."

Joseph was overjoyed to see his brothers, and after the shock wore off, they were happy to see him. As his dreams had predicted, Joseph's brothers had indeed bowed down before him many times. However, Joseph's joy came not from his position of authority, but from forgiving his brothers.

Genesis 43–44, 45:1–14

The time came when Joseph's brothers had to return to Egypt for food. Reluctantly, their father let them take Benjamin, so hopefully they could all come home together. Once again, they were brought before the governor of Egypt, Soon after, they were dining with him, still unaware of who he was. Joseph had his silver cup placed in Benjamin's sack. This would be his final test. Accused of stealing, Benjamin was going to be put in prison. His brother Judah told Joseph to take him instead. At this, Joseph revealed his true identity.

Hard Times for Israel

There was a great time of joy for Joseph and all his family when they were together again. They all moved to Egypt, and their family grew larger and larger. As the years passed, a new leader of Egypt came who did not remember Joseph and his wisdom. Because of the new king's fear, he took Joseph's descendants and made them slaves. Nevertheless, God's promise and plans for Israel would come to pass.

So, Jacob's sons returned to him and told him that Joseph was alive. Not only was he alive, he was the governor of Egypt. At first, Jacob did not believe them. When he saw the carts Joseph had sent to carry him back to Egypt, he was overjoyed. He would see his beloved son again!

The entire family moved to Egypt and prospered there for many years. Before he died, Jacob blessed each of his sons and predicted what would happen to them in the future. His words to Judah are worth remembering:

"The scepter will not depart from Judah, nor the ruler's staff from his descendants, until the coming of the one to whom it belongs, the one whom all nations will honor" (Genesis 49:10; NLT).

As time passed, the sons of Jacob multiplied into 12 large tribes. A new Egyptian king came to power that felt no loyalty to Joseph's family. In fact, he feared them. If the Israelites continued to multiply, they might rise up and fight against him. So he made them slaves instead of citizens, just as God had told Abraham would happen (Genesis 15:13).

They were forced into hard labor and built the cities of Pithom and Rameses brick by brick. It was backbreaking work. The Egyptians made their lives miserable.

Pharaoh believed if he worked the slaves hard enough, they would be too tired to keep having children. Yet the harder he worked them, the more children they had. God had promised Abraham that He would multiply Abraham's offspring (Genesis 22:17). Despite Pharaoh's efforts, that is exactly what happened.

The king was unaware he was battling against the God of Israel, but he would soon find out.

➳ *Genesis 45:25–28, 46*

➳ *Exodus 1*

Saved Out of the Water

The king of Egypt had tried various methods of controlling the growth of the Israelite population. None of them had worked. So, in a last ditch effort, he ordered the Egyptian people to throw all the baby boys born to an Israelite into the Nile River.

Around this time, a son was born to one of the slaves. Her name was Jochebed. She and her husband, Amram, had two other children named Aaron and Miriam. Jochebed hid her baby from the Egyptians for as long as she could. When she realized she could hide him no longer, she placed him in a waterproof basket and set him gently in the river. She prayed someone would save him.

Miriam stood nearby to see what would happen. Soon, Pharaoh's daughter came down to the river to bathe and found the baby. She felt sorry for him and decided to adopt him. She told Miriam to find him a nursemaid. So Miriam went and brought the baby's mother, Jochebed. "I will pay you to take this child and nurse him for me," the princess said.

Imagine Jochebed's joy — not only would her son live, she would be allowed to care for him! When he was weaned, she took him to the princess, who named him Moses, which means "saved out of the water."

Just as God had spared Noah and his family out of the water, He spared this infant child who floated down the Nile River in a tiny ark made of rushes and reeds.

Exodus 1–2

Numbers 26:59

Acts 7:20–22

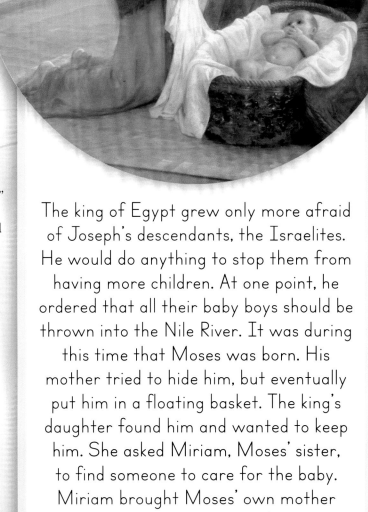

The king of Egypt grew only more afraid of Joseph's descendants, the Israelites. He would do anything to stop them from having more children. At one point, he ordered that all their baby boys should be thrown into the Nile River. It was during this time that Moses was born. His mother tried to hide him, but eventually put him in a floating basket. The king's daughter found him and wanted to keep him. She asked Miriam, Moses' sister, to find someone to care for the baby. Miriam brought Moses' own mother to feed and nurture him as he grew.

Holy Ground

Moses was raised as a royal prince of Egypt, but he knew who his true people were. He also knew they were being mistreated. One day when he was older, he noticed an Egyptian severely beating one of his countrymen. Moses came to the man's defense and ended up killing the Egyptian. He thought the Israelites would appreciate his help, but they did not. Instead, they said, "Who made you a ruler and a judge over us?" When the king found out what happened, he wanted to kill Moses. So Moses fled through the wilderness to the land of Midian, where he found work as a shepherd.

One day many years later, Moses took his sheep to graze near Mount Sinai. In the distance, he noticed a bush that appeared to be on fire. He found it odd that the bush did not burn up, so he walked over to investigate. God spoke to Moses from inside the fire, saying, "Do not come any closer. Take off your sandals, for the place where you are standing is holy ground. I am the God of your father, the God of Abraham, the God of Isaac, and the God of Jacob."

When Moses heard the voice of God, he covered his face in fear because he realized he was in the presence of God's glory.

Then the LORD told Moses He had plans to rescue His people in Egypt. He wanted Moses to lead them out of their slavery. He told Moses to go back to the king and ask him to release them, but Moses protested. After all, he was wanted for murder in Egypt, and his people had rejected his help once before. He did not think anyone would listen to him. "Who am I that I should go and bring the Israelites out of Egypt? What if no one believes me?" he said.

Moses needed to know that his success would come by God's power and blessing, not by his own abilities. So, the LORD told him to throw his staff on the ground, and it became a snake. Then the LORD told him to pick it up by the tail, and it became a staff again. "They will believe you when they see this," the LORD said. "And if they don't, I will give you other signs to prove that I am with you."

God told Moses that one day he would lead Israel back to this very spot. Moses continued to protest until God offered to send his brother, Aaron, to help him. Finally, he agreed to go.

Exodus 2:11–23, 3–4

Acts 7:20-34

Moses grew up in the royal family of Egypt. However, he knew the slaves who suffered there were his relatives. One day he tried to stop an Egyptian from hurting one of the Israelites. In this fight, he killed the Egyptian. Fearing for his life, he ran into the wilderness. While tending sheep near a mountain called Sinai, Moses heard God calling him from a burning bush. God was going to use Moses to lead His people out of Egypt. God would work signs and wonders through Moses. His brother, Aaron, would help him overcome his self-doubt.

Thread of Hope

Jacob was born grasping his brother's heel. He had taken his brother's birthright and blessing and was not above deceiving his own father. However, he had met his match in Laban. Not only did Laban instruct Leah to pretend to be her sister, he had lied to Jacob and taken advantage of him for many years. Some would say that Jacob got what he deserved. In truth, God allows us to experience the consequences of sin so that we can see for ourselves the end result of man's disobedience.

God had a plan for Jacob's life, but it would require a changed heart. So He called Jacob back to Canaan — He called him home. The journey would not be easy, for Jacob would have to face enemies along the way. In typical Jacob style, he planned to sneak away from one and bribe the other. After all, he had always schemed his way out of trouble before.

Along the way, he got into a wrestling match with none other than the angel of God. He struggled with Him throughout the night. Jacob's hip was injured in the fight, leaving him physically disabled. More importantly, he had come to the end of himself. Only in realizing his spiritual disability could he come to understand his need to rely on God instead of himself.

Then the most amazing thing happened. God blessed him and gave him a new name, one that spoke of a future. It was a future that required dependence on God. Jacob came away from that experience a changed man. He knew he was too weak to face his enemies alone, but with God, he could face anything. The next morning he set out to meet his brother, limping as he went.

Jacob's sons would also go on to wrestle with God. The years following their arrival in Canaan would give each of them many opportunities to come to terms with their own sinful natures as well. The ten oldest sons hated Joseph. So much so that they sold him to slave traders. With an ironic act of grace, Joseph ended up saving his long-lost family from starvation.

Joseph gave all the credit to God, saying, *"You meant evil against me, but God meant it for good"* (Genesis 50:20). Years of slavery and prison had given Joseph the opportunity to face his own sinful nature, and learn to depend on God.

Many generations later, God revealed Himself to another descendant of Jacob. He called Moses out of hiding and into the plan of God. Moses was a little slow to accept God's plan for his life, but as you will soon read, he did put his faith into action and remained faithful to God until his death.

de·pen·dence	needing the help of another
bless·ing	special favor or gifts given by God
faith·ful	to remain loyal and true to another

Let My People Go!

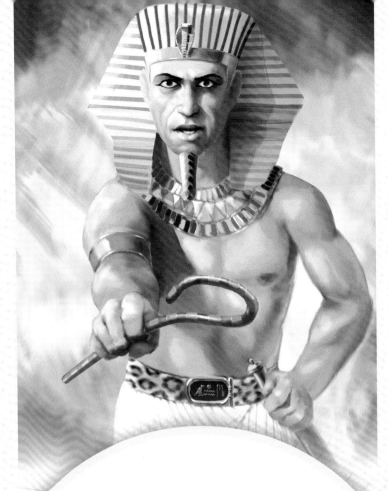

As promised, the LORD sent Aaron to the wilderness to meet up with Moses. It must have been good for these two brothers to see each other again after so many years. Moses told Aaron everything God had said, and together, they went to the leaders of Israel. "The God of our ancestors has promised to free us from slavery and lead us to a land flowing with milk and honey," Aaron told them. The leaders were thankful. God had heard their cry for help!

Now, Egypt was a land of many false gods, and the pharaoh was the religious leader of the country. He knew all about the Egyptian gods, but he knew nothing about the God of Israel. So, when Moses and Aaron approached him and said, "This is what the LORD, the God of Israel, says: Let my people go," he was angry and offended. How dare they make demands of the king from a God he did not know or represent! He was so mad that he instructed his slavedrivers to work the Israelites even harder.

Then Moses asked the LORD, "Why have you brought trouble on Israel? Is this why you sent me? Ever since I went to the king to speak in your name, he has made their lives even harder, and you have not rescued your people at all." God responded:

"Now you shall see what I will do to Pharaoh. For with a strong hand he will let them go, and with a strong hand he will drive them out of his land. … I am the LORD. I appeared to Abraham, to Isaac, and to Jacob, as God Almighty, but by My name LORD I was not known to them. I have also established My covenant with them, to give them the land of Canaan, the land of their pilgrimage, in which they were strangers. And I have also heard the groaning of the children of Israel whom the Egyptians keep in bondage, and I have remembered My covenant" (Exodus 6:1–5; NKJV).

Exodus 3:16–17, 4:28–30, 5, 6:1–5

Moses and his brother Aaron began talking about all that God had promised. They then came to the leaders of the Israelites to tell them of God's desire to free them from slavery. This had been their prayer for many years. Egypt was also a land of false gods. The king did not wish to hear about the God of Moses, nor did he want to free the Israelite slaves. In fact, Pharaoh made sure the slaves were forced to work harder so they would blame Moses and Aaron.

The One True God

The Israelites who were living at this time had been slaves their whole lives. It was all they had ever known. Knowledge of the God of their ancestors would have been passed down to them, but they had also been exposed to the false gods of Egypt. They may have even worshiped them. The time had come for them to place their faith and their future in the one true God.

He told Moses to say to them:

"I am the LORD; I will bring you out from under the burdens of the Egyptians, I will rescue you from their bondage, and I will redeem you with an outstretched arm and with great judgments. I will take you as My people, and I will be your God. Then you shall know that I am the LORD your God who brings you out from under the burdens of the Egyptians. And I will bring you into the land which I swore to give to Abraham, Isaac, and Jacob; and I will give it to you as a heritage: I am the LORD" (Exodus 6:6–8; NKJV).

The people did not listen. They were not ready to trust that God would take them back to Canaan. Instead, they were sad and angry because their lives had become even more difficult since Moses and Aaron arrived.

In the days that followed, God demonstrated His great power by performing many miracles that came in the form of various plagues. Moses asked Pharaoh nine more times to let the people go. Each time, Pharaoh said, *"No."* So, God performed even bigger miracles. At first, the king's own "wise men" and sorcerers were able to perform similar acts, but it soon became apparent that they were outmatched.

Each of God's miracles are worthy of a book of their own. He turned the Nile River into blood and sent plagues of frogs, gnats, and flies to cover the land. He took the lives of the Egyptians' livestock, sent a terrible sickness of boils, destroyed their crops with hail and locusts, and sent a deep darkness to cover the land. While all these horrible things happened in Egypt, not one person, animal, or home had been harmed in the area where the Israelites lived.

With each miracle, the Israelites saw that the gods of Egypt actually had no power at all. However, the one true God — He was something altogether different. They had probably heard how He had once rescued Noah and his family from a mighty Flood of judgment. Now, they saw that power with their own eyes, and their faith began to grow.

Exodus 5–10

Hundreds of years before, God had called Abraham to follow Him, promising that his descendants would be God's people. Now God's people lived in slavery to Egypt, but He was wanting to show them who He really was. At first, they grew angry at God because they were being oppressed even more. Then God began working miracles to show His power, both to the ruler of Egypt and to the Israelites. They had heard of God and His wonders, but now they were seeing these wonders with their own eyes. Awful plagues came upon Egypt, but none of God's people were hurt by them.

Passed Over

Passed Over

Pharaoh was stubborn, and he refused to let the Israelites go. So God would send one final and devastating plague. This one would be so painful that the citizens of Egypt would beg the Israelites to leave. Moses and Aaron told the king, "Tonight, every firstborn in Egypt will die. From the firstborn son of the king, to the son of those in prison. Even the firstborn of the livestock will die."

Moses instructed the Israelites to prepare for a long journey. Then, each family was to select a perfect lamb, one without any defect, and sacrifice it at twilight. They were to place some of the lamb's blood on the doorframe of their home as a sign that those within were protected. The lamb acted as a substitute for the firstborn son. Any home that was not covered by the blood of the lamb would lose their firstborn son that night. Then the lamb was to be roasted and eaten quickly with unleavened bread and bitter herbs.

The plague began at midnight. Cries were heard throughout Egypt, for there was not a house without someone dead. From the worst criminal in prison to Pharaoh himself, every Egyptian family lost their firstborn son. Whereas the Israelites were spared. The plague had passed over them.

Pharaoh called for Moses and Aaron in the middle of the night. "Take your people and go, but please bless me before you leave." This plague had shaken his pride and resolve. No doubt he had also gained a little fear and respect for the one true God, though it did not last long.

The people of Egypt were also anxious for the Israelites to leave. They even gave them clothing and articles of silver and gold. So Abraham's descendants left Egypt, having gone from slavery to freedom, and from poverty to plenty in a matter of hours.

They were headed to the Promised Land.

Exodus 11–12

One final plague would come upon Egypt. This would take the life of every firstborn son throughout the land, human and animal. Yet God would keep His people safe. The Israelites were to kill a perfect lamb and spread some of its blood over the doorway to their homes so the plague would pass over them. Then they were to cook the lamb and eat it as a special meal. At midnight, the plague came, and the cries of the Egyptians were heard throughout the land. The king called Moses and Aaron to tell them he wanted them to leave with all the Israelites. God's power had broken through the king's pride.

Free at Last

*N*ow, the shortest route to Canaan was through Philistine country, but the Philistines were known to be ruthless warriors. So God led them on a longer and more difficult route through the desert in order to avoid an attack. By day, the LORD went ahead of Israel in a pillar of cloud, and by night, in a pillar of fire. In this way they could visibly see that God was with them, offering them His protective covering and His guiding light.

After a few days, Pharaoh had second thoughts. "What have we done, letting all those slaves get away?" So he gathered his army and set out in pursuit. The Israelites were approaching the Red Sea when the king's army caught up with them. They panicked and cried out to Moses, "What have you done to us? Why didn't you listen when we told you, 'Leave us alone; let us serve the Egyptians'? We would rather be slaves than die here!"

Moses said, "Don't be afraid. You will never see these Egyptians again. Have faith and watch the LORD fight for you."

Then the pillar of cloud and fire moved between Israel and the Egyptian soldiers. On the Egyptian side it was so dark they could not see how to proceed. On the Israelite side it was light. Then Moses stretched out his hand over the sea. Miraculously, God drove the water back so that there was a path of dry ground, with a wall of water on both sides. The people of Israel safely crossed the seabed throughout the night. In the morning, the Egyptians followed, but God released His hold on the water, and the sea went back to its place, drowning the entire army.

There was quite a celebration on the other side of the sea with singing, dancing, and shouts of praise. God had delivered them!

Exodus 13:17–22, 14

Isaiah 51:10

The Israelites had been slaves for generations. Now they were walking away from Egypt in freedom. God took them into the desert, guiding them by day with a pillar of cloud and by night with a pillar of fire. Soon the Egyptian king regretted letting them go. He came for them with an army to bring them back by force. God would again show His power. Moses prayed and stretched out his hand over the sea, and God parted the water so His people could walk across on dry ground. When the Egyptians tried to cross, the waters fell back over them, drowning them all.

Fire and Commandments

*M*oses led Israel into the desert and toward Mount Sinai, the place where God had spoken to him from the fire. Though they had been slaves, this generation of Israelites had not experienced drought or famine in Egypt. It had been a fertile land with plenty of water provided by the Nile River.

Life in the desert was completely different. Food and water were not plentiful. Israel would have to learn to trust God to provide for them. This proved to be a difficult lesson to learn. There was a lot of arguing and complaining even as God provided both water and food. They ate manna throughout the time they were in the desert. This was a miraculous provision of daily bread that was referred to as the "food of angels."

After they arrived at Mt. Sinai, they set up camp. Then Moses walked up the mountain to hear from God. The LORD told him to go back down and relay this message to the Israelites:

"You yourselves have seen what I did to the Egyptians, and how I bore you on eagles' wings and brought you to myself. Now therefore, if you will indeed obey my voice and keep my covenant, you shall be my treasured possession among all peoples, for all the earth is mine; and you shall be to me a kingdom of priests and a holy nation" (Exodus 19:4–6).

The people told Moses that they would do everything the LORD said. Then the LORD told Moses He wanted the people of Israel to hear His voice for themselves.

Three days later, a thick cloud covered the mountain. There was thunder, lightning, and a loud trumpet blast. Everyone in the camp trembled. Then Moses led them to the base of Mt. Sinai, which was covered in smoke because the LORD had descended on it in fire. The mountain shook and the sound of the trumpet grew louder and louder. The people could hear God's voice from the fire, but they were forbidden from going up the mountain. The one true God was not like the idols from Egypt. Those had been mere statues. Their God was holy and powerful.

God gave Israel special commandments, or laws, to follow. The Ten Commandments were later inscribed on tablets of stone. Israel promised to abide by these laws, but it did not take long for them to break their promise. Had they been able to live by God's commandments, they would have looked different from the nations around them. They would have been a shining example of God's goodness.

Exodus 19–20

Deuteronomy 5–6

As the Israelites continued through the desert, they realized how dry and barren it was. Egypt had plenty of food and water. Now God's people would need to learn how to depend on Him for everything. Though they complained constantly, God continually provided for all their physical needs. He also wanted them to know Him in a deeper way, as Moses did. At the mountain of Sinai, God's presence was felt in smoke and fire. God gave them laws to help guide them in justice and love. These would help them be a light of God's holiness in the world.

A New Way to Worship

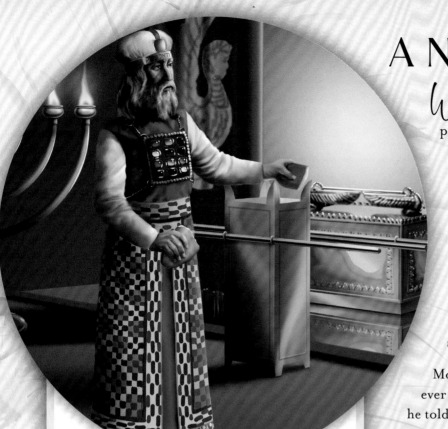

With these commandments came a new religious system. It was a system that required sacrifice to atone for sin. God knew that people would not be able to keep the law perfectly. This was not its purpose. He gave them the law so they would understand they could not be perfect. Everyone sins from time to time.

There were several different types of sacrifices in this system, each with its own purpose. For the time being, the blood of animals would atone for people's sin (Exodus 30:10; Leviticus 4:20), but these sacrifices would have to be made over and over again. It is very important to understand that it was not faith in the animal's blood that atoned for sin. Instead, it was faith in God Himself, who accepted the animal's blood as a substitute.

Moses knew that without a true love for God, Israel had no hope of ever obeying Him. True love and worship must begin in the heart. So he told them:

"Hear, O Israel: The LORD our God, the LORD is one. You shall love the LORD your God with all your heart and with all your soul and with all your might" (Deuteronomy 6:4–5).

God also told Moses to build a special tent for worship, called a tabernacle. Aaron and his descendants from the tribe of Levi would be the priests of the tabernacle. The Ten Commandments were placed inside a box called the Ark of the Covenant. This box represented God's presence and His promise. It was placed behind a special curtain inside the tabernacle, in an area called the Holy of Holies.

When the tabernacle was completed, the pillar of cloud that had traveled with Israel since they left Egypt settled over it. *... and the glory of the LORD filled the tabernacle. And Moses was not able to enter the tent of meeting because the cloud settled on it, and the glory of the LORD filled the tabernacle... For the cloud of the LORD was on the tabernacle by day, and fire was in it by night, in the sight of all the house of Israel throughout all their journeys* (Exodus 40:34–35, 38).

Heaven and earth met inside the Holy of Holies, for God's spirit dwelled there. No one was allowed to enter the Holy of Holies except the high priest — and then only once a year on the Day of Atonement. On this day, the priest would offer a special sacrifice for the sins of Israel.

➢ *Exodus 15, 19–20, 25, 30, 34, 40*

➢ *Deuteronomy 6*

The laws given to the Israelites were meant to guide their relationship with God and with others. The laws taught them about sin and their need for salvation, not how they might live perfect lives. The focus of the laws came down to loving God in every way possible. True love and worship always begin in the heart. Soon they would have a special tent created for worship called the tabernacle.

So Much to Learn

Israel needed time to learn how to live and work together as a free nation, so they camped at Mt. Sinai for around two years. During this time, they received the law, built the tabernacle, and entered into a covenant with the LORD, whereby they promised to trust and obey Him.

In the second month of the second year, the cloud lifted from over the tabernacle. That meant it was time to move on. There were over 600,000 men of fighting age, not including the priests. Some historians estimate there were over two million people all together. It was an exciting time and must have been quite a sight to see an entire nation of people walking through the wilderness. Off they went, finally heading for the Promised Land of Canaan.

Sadly, it did not take long before they began to break their promise to God. Instead of trusting Him, they began to argue and complain. They argued with one another and with Moses. Like spoiled children, they complained when they were thirsty, or hungry, or hot, or tired. Each day seemed to bring a new struggle.

Many of these people wanted to return to Egypt. They would rather be slaves than not know what was coming next. They had great fear, little faith, and much to learn on this journey.

Finally, they arrived on the outskirts of Canaan, and Moses sent scouts to explore this new land. One man was selected from each of the 12 tribes. He instructed them to inspect the territory and report back. Was the land fertile? Who was living there? How big were their armies? What was the best route to take?

Numbers 1:46, 10—12, 13:1—24

After staying near the mountain of Sinai for just over two years, it was time for God's people to move on. Possibly two million or more Israelites began walking toward the Promised Land. Though they were free and saw God's miracles so often now, they were constantly whining and complaining. Some even wanted to return to Egypt where they had been slaves. When they got to the outskirts of Canaan, Moses sent one spy from each of the 12 tribes to explore the land. They would see if the land was fertile and if those living there could possibly stop them from entering God's Promised Land.

A Giant Decision

After 40 days, the scouts returned. They brought back samples of fruit — pomegranates, figs, and a bunch of grapes so large that two of them carried it on a pole between them! It was indeed a beautiful and bountiful land.

The men began to give an account of their journey. Caleb said, "We can easily conquer the land. Let's go!"

Joshua agreed with Caleb, but the other ten argued, saying, "We can't go up against them! They are stronger than we are — and so big that we felt like grasshoppers next to them!" That night the entire community wept aloud. Whom should they trust? Caleb and Joshua — or the other men? Their choice was whether or not to trust what God had promised.

Sadly, they made the wrong choice. "If only we had died in Egypt! Or in this wilderness! Why is the Lord bringing us to this land only to let us fall by the sword? Our wives and children will be taken as plunder. Wouldn't it be better for us to go back to Egypt? Let's choose a leader and go back," they said.

They had come so close. Close enough to see what God had promised. Close enough to taste the fruit of the land. Yet they did not have the faith to take it. After all that God had done for them, after all He had brought them through, these people still did not trust Him. God was angry, but Moses asked Him to forgive them. So, the LORD did. He said,

"I have pardoned, according to your word. But truly, as I live, and as all the earth shall be filled with the glory of the LORD, none of the men who have seen my glory and my signs that I did in Egypt and in the wilderness, and yet have put me to the test these ten times and have not obeyed my voice, shall see the land that I swore to give to their fathers" (Numbers 14:20–23).

Then he struck down the ten scouts who had caused the rebellion and sent everyone else back into the wilderness. They would wander there for 40 years, one year for each of the 40 days the scouts had explored the land.

Numbers 13:23–33, 14

Twelve spies went into Canaan to see if the Israelites might be able to take this land of promise. After 40 days, they returned with their report and some of the abundant fruit. Joshua and Caleb were filled with faith in God's protection and guidance. They said that the land was beautiful and that the Israelites should enter it at once. However, the other ten spies saw only the strength of the people in the land. These spies convinced everyone that they would die if they tried to take what God had promised them. Because of them, the Israelites would wander the desert for 40 more years.

Wilderness Lessons

The next 40 years was a time of great testing. Israel's faith wavered, and they grumbled constantly. One time, they had stopped for the night in a place that had no water. They complained, "Why did you bring us here to die of thirst? We would be better off going back to Egypt."

So, God told Moses and Aaron to speak to a certain rock — and it would pour out water before Israel's eyes. Moses was frustrated. He was tired of their constant whining. Why couldn't they see that God had always provided? He angrily struck the rock twice with his staff and said, "Listen, you rebels, must we bring you water out of this rock?" Water did indeed gush out from the rock, but God was not pleased. Instead of simply speaking to the rock, Moses and Aaron had drawn attention to themselves by striking it in anger.

"Because you did not trust in me enough to honor me as holy in the sight of the Israelites, you will not bring this community into the land I give them," God said.

Neither Moses nor Aaron would be allowed to enter the Promised Land! That had to hurt. Now, they could have reacted like their countrymen and complained that God's judgment was too harsh, but they did not. They humbly accepted the consequences. They understood that God's holiness is not something to take lightly.

In the future, Israel would have another chance to enter the Promised Land. So Moses spent the last years of his life preparing them for that day. He reminded them how God's faithful love, presence, and power had always provided. He told them to be strong and courageous. He warned them not to become prideful. God would not give them the land because they were righteous, for they were not. He would do it because the nations who currently lived there were wicked. It was God's righteousness that would win the day, not theirs. Finally, he went over all the commands and laws of God and reminded Israel of their covenant with Him. Their future would hold either blessings or curses. It was their choice. He said:

"I call heaven and earth to witness against you today, that I have set before you life and death, blessing and curse. Therefore choose life, that you and your offspring may live, loving the LORD your God, obeying his voice and holding fast to him, for he is your life and length of days, that you may dwell in the land that the LORD swore to your fathers, to Abraham, to Isaac, and to Jacob, to give them" (Deuteronomy 30:19–20).

≫ *Numbers 15–21*

≫ *Deuteronomy 9:1–6, 28–30*

Forty years is a long time to wander a desert. This is what happened to the Israelites because they doubted God's ability to protect them. As one might expect, the people grumbled and complained constantly about Moses' and Aaron's leadership. At one point, the people needed water. God told Moses to speak to a rock so that water would pour out. In his anger, Moses struck the rock with his staff. Because he disobeyed, God said he would not be able to enter the Promised Land, though he did see it before his death. In his last days, he instructed the people how to serve and honor God through His covenant with them.

Thread of Hope

The people of Israel had fled to Egypt, a powerful and prosperous nation. It was also a land of many false gods. They had gotten comfortable with those false gods and made Egypt their home. They settled in. Over time, what had started out as a place of refuge had become a prison. This is how Satan's schemes often work. God had known this would happen (Genesis 15:13), and at exactly the right time, He intervened in history again.

The rescue of Israel from slavery is a story of many miracles, not the least of which is the life of their reluctant deliverer. Moses was born in troubled times. By Pharaoh's law, he should have been drowned at birth. Instead, he was raised as a son in Pharaoh's house.

His name means "saved out of the water." Moses had indeed been rescued from the Nile River as a baby. He would go on to lead an entire nation through the water of the Red Sea shortly before the enemy who chased them drowned. Moses was God's chosen vessel to lead Israel out of slavery, and before he died, God allowed him to see the Promised Land from a distance.

Through Moses, God had called His people to return to Him. Then He proved, beyond a shadow of a doubt, that the false gods of Egypt were powerless. Each of the ten plagues had been chosen to correspond to one of their "gods," and the LORD made a mockery of them. There should have been no doubt in anyone's mind, Israelite or Egyptian, that there was only one true God — the LORD, the God of Israel — for they had all seen His glory.

God traveled with Israel into the wilderness, where He protected them and provided for them. He demonstrated His power and His patience and gave them glimpses of His holiness. He spoke to them from the fire of His glory. He gave them instructions for life and for worship. He entered into a covenant with them. God proved Himself over and over again.

The rest was up to them. The land was promised, but they would have to fight for it. During their years in the wilderness, an entire generation of Israelites died — those who had refused to place their faith in God. They had been given the same opportunity to "choose life" as everyone else, but their hearts were hard toward Him.

We can take many lessons from this story, the most important being a reminder of the two paths we must all choose from. One leads to life and the other to death.

re·deem	to buy back, or to free from captivity
slav·er·y	a state of being controlled by another person, system, or thing
i·dol·a·try	anything we trust or serve apart from God in hopes of getting what we want

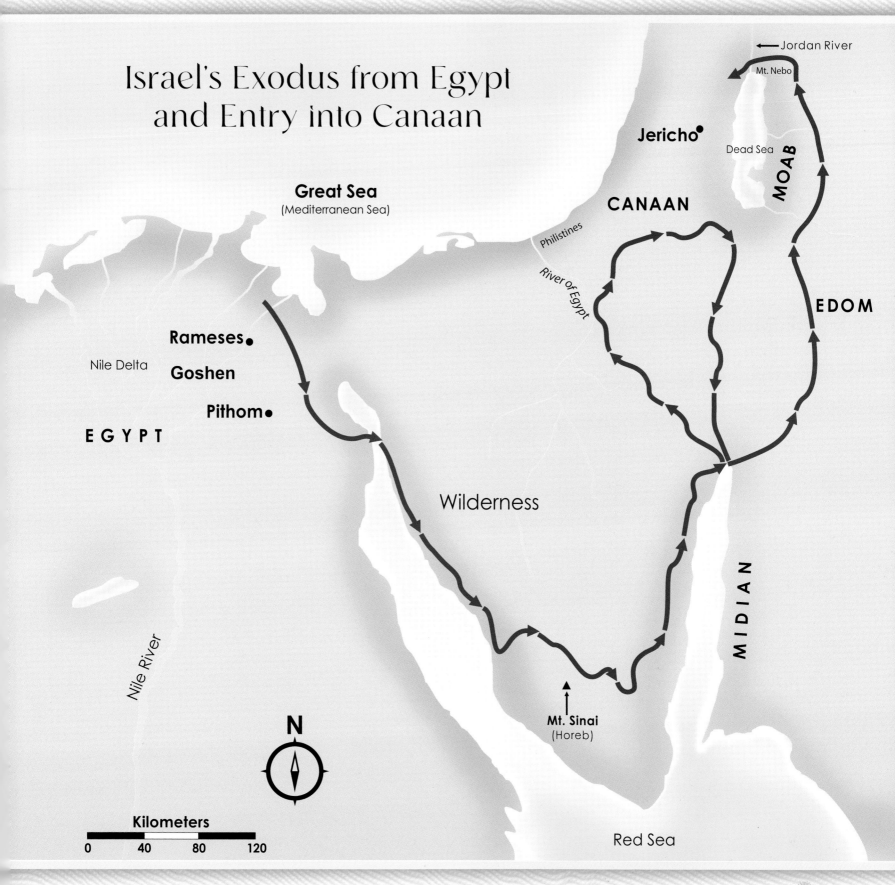

Israel's Exodus from Egypt and Entry into Canaan

Jordan River

Mt. Nebo

Jericho

Dead Sea

Great Sea
(Mediterranean Sea)

MOAB

CANAAN

Philistines

River of Egypt

EDOM

Rameses

Nile Delta

Goshen

Pithom

EGYPT

Wilderness

MIDIAN

Nile River

Mt. Sinai
(Horeb)

N

Kilometers

0   40   80   120

Red Sea

Joshua Conquers Jericho

Joshua Conquers Jericho

Joshua was Moses' friend and right-hand man for many years. After Moses died, the LORD told Joshua to prepare the Israelites to enter the Promised Land. "No one will be able to stand against you," He said. "As I was with Moses, so I will be with you; I will never leave you or forsake you. Be strong and courageous. Be careful to obey my laws, and you will be successful wherever you go."

The first battle would be at Jericho, and Joshua sent out two scouts ahead of the army. The king of Jericho heard that these spies were in his city, for they had been spotted at the home of a woman named Rahab. He sent her a message saying, "The men you are entertaining are spies, hand them over to us!" Instead, Rahab hid the spies under some stalks of flax and told the king's men that they had already left.

Later that night, she told the men that the people of Jericho were terrified of the God of Israel. They had heard about all He had done to save His people since they had left Egypt. Her house was built into the city wall, so she took a rope and let it out the window so the men could escape. The men agreed to spare Rahab and her family when they attacked as long as a scarlet rope was hanging out of her window when they returned.

In order to reach Jericho, Israel would have to cross the Jordan River, which was at flood stage. Joshua told the priests to go in first, carrying the Ark of the Covenant. The Ark reminded them that God would go before them. As soon as the priests put their feet in the river, the water from upstream stopped flowing. The Israelites walked across the riverbed on dry ground, just as they had done when they left Egypt.

When the kings of the nearby cities heard that God had dried up the Jordan River, they were afraid to fight against Israel. At Jericho, the gates to the city had been closed and locked. No one went out and no one was allowed in.

The LORD gave Joshua a battle plan. "Have the army march around the city one time a day for six days. Have priests march with them, carrying trumpets and the Ark of the Covenant. On the seventh day, march around the city seven times, with the priests blowing the trumpets."

The army followed God's instructions, and after the seventh round, Joshua commanded them, "Shout, for the LORD has given us victory over this city!" So the soldiers gave a loud shout, and the walls of Jericho collapsed. The army charged in and took the city, burning it to the ground. Out of all the citizens of Jericho, only Rahab and her family were spared.

Deuteronomy 34

Joshua 1–6

Joshua became the new leader of Israel after Moses died. Soon he would be leading the Israelites into their first battle at a city named Jericho. He sent two spies into the walled city. These spies met a woman named Rahab, who knew that those in the city were full of fear of God's people. Before they attacked, God led His people through the Jordan River, as He had led them through the Red Sea. Then He gave them the city of Jericho after they marched around its walls for seven days.

Tribes of Israel

Jacob		
	Leah	Reuben
		Simeon
		Levi
		Judah
		Issachar
		Zebulun
	Zilpah	Gad
		Asher
	Bilhah	Dan
		Naphtali
	Rachel	Joseph
		Benjamin

Before he died, Moses had allotted land to the tribes of Reuben, Gad, and half of the tribe of Manasseh on the east side of the Jordan River (Numbers 32:33). In chapters 13-19 of Joshua, the other tribes received their allotment on the west side, except for the tribe of Levi (Deuteronomy 10:9; Joshua 13:14). The land noted for Ephraim and Manasseh represents Joseph's portion as they were his sons.

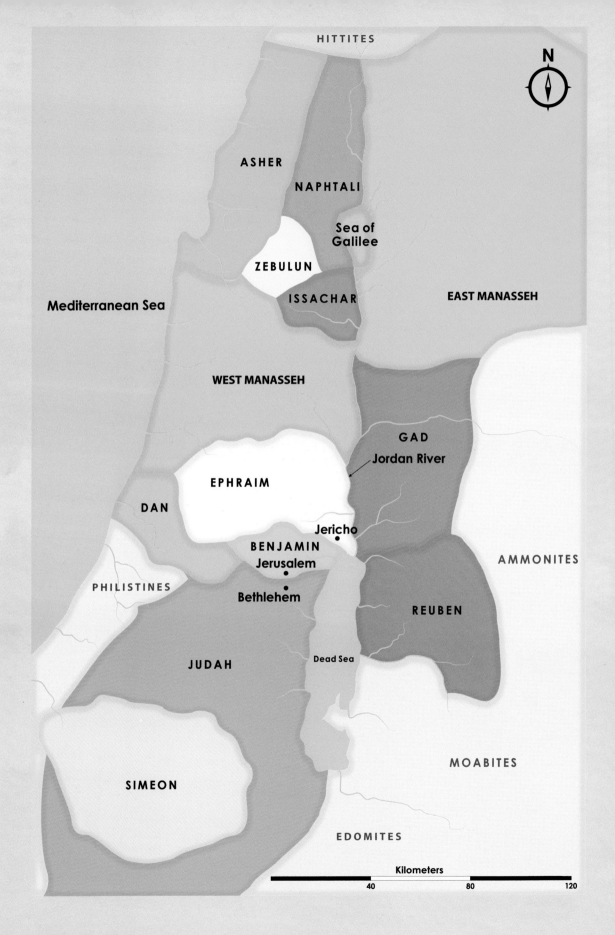

HITTITES

N

ASHER

NAPHTALI

Sea of Galilee

ZEBULUN

ISSACHAR

EAST MANASSEH

Mediterranean Sea

WEST MANASSEH

GAD

Jordan River

EPHRAIM

DAN

Jericho

BENJAMIN

Jerusalem

AMMONITES

PHILISTINES

Bethlehem

REUBEN

Dead Sea

JUDAH

MOABITES

SIMEON

EDOMITES

Kilometers

40   80   120

Taking the Land

After their victory at Jericho, Joshua and his army set out to take the rest of the Promised Land, and God was with them. He had given the Canaanites 400 years to turn from their wicked ways, but they had not. During all the years that Israel had been in Egypt, the Canaanites had practiced evil. So the LORD gave their land to Israel.

It took several years, but Israel finally conquered enough land to gain control of the region. Then the LORD gave them a period of rest from war. During this time, the land was divided among the tribes of Israel, and the people settled in. They built homes and planted crops. They finally had a homeland, but there was still work to do. Joshua and his army had not completely driven the Canaanites from the land. There were still enemies to fight. There were still idols to destroy.

When Joshua was too old to go to war, he called the nation together. "The LORD will give you victory over the rest of your enemies if you remain faithful to him. Be very strong; be careful to obey his laws," he said. "Do not mix with these people; do not call on their gods. You are to hold fast to the LORD your God, as you have until now. He has driven out great and powerful nations before you. No one has been able to withstand you because the LORD fights for you. So be very careful to love the LORD your God."

Israel did remain faithful for a time. However, things fell apart after Joshua and all the leaders from his generation died. Sadly, instead of destroying the remaining idols in the land, the next generation began to worship them. Soon they were taking part in wicked acts, including human sacrifice. God had wanted to protect Israel from these evil ideas, but He allowed them to suffer the consequences of their choices. God withheld His protection, and they fell into the hands of their enemies. During these periods of oppression, Israel was terrorized by the remaining Canaanites.

When things became unbearable, Israel would ask God for help, and God would send them a deliverer. These deliverers were known as judges. They would lead Israel to victory, which would be followed by a period of peace, but the people eventually returned to idol worship. This cycle of sin, consequences, repentance, and deliverance would be repeated many times for the next 400 years, for *everyone did what was right in his own eyes* (Judges 21:25).

Thus the LORD gave to Israel all the land that he swore to give to their fathers. And they took possession of it, and they settled there (Joshua 21:43).

- Numbers 33:51–52
- Deuteronomy 7, 34:9
- Joshua 1–24
- Judges 1–21
- Psalm 105

The city of Jericho was only the first of many wicked cities to fall into the hands of God's people. Soon the land of Canaan belonged to the Israelites, and the LORD gave them rest from war. This land was divided up among the tribes, and they began to thrive here. Even though there were enemies who still lived around them. After Joshua died, the people went through cycles of sin and repentance. When the people pursued wicked things, their enemies would overwhelm them. When they called on God, He would deliver them.

Women Warriors

A wicked Canaanite commander named Sisera had been oppressing Israel for 20 years. A woman named Deborah was the judge of Israel at the time. God told Deborah that soon they would have victory over Sisera and his army. She called for Israel's army commander, Barak. Barak was willing to fight but only if Deborah came with him. She agreed, but let him know that he would not get credit for the victory. Instead, the honor would go to a woman, and that is what happened. A woman named Jael took Sisera's life and ended his oppression of Israel. Then they had peace for 40 years.

One of Israel's judges was a woman named Deborah. She held court under a palm tree in the hill country of Ephraim, where the Israelites would bring their disputes. During her lifetime, Israel was being tormented by Sisera, the commander of Canaan's army.

He was a cruel man who had oppressed Israel for 20 years. He commanded 900 chariots and used them to terrorize the people of Israel. So they cried out to the LORD.

Then Deborah sent for Barak, the commander of Israel's army, and told him, "The God of Israel commands you to take ten thousand men and lead them up to Mount Tabor. The LORD will give you victory over Sisera."

Barak replied, "If you go with me, I will go; but if you don't go with me, I won't go."

"I will certainly go with you, but the road you are taking will bring you no honor, because the LORD will be selling Sisera into the hand of a woman," Deborah said.

So Deborah bravely went to war alongside Barak and the army of Israel. They attacked Sisera's troops at the Kishon River and were victorious. Not a single Canaanite soldier was left alive that day except Sisera, who had survived by escaping on foot. He had hidden in the tent of a woman named Jael. Thinking he was safe, he soon fell asleep. Jael killed him as he lay there.

Then the land had peace from war for 40 years. Once again, God had shown His faithfulness to Israel, and Deborah's prophecy had come to pass. Sisera had died at the hands of a woman.

Yet Israel's cycle of sin continued, and before long, they were enslaved by the Philistines.

Judges 4–5

Strong but Not Wise

Another of Israel's judges was a man named Samson. He was the son of Manoah, a man from the territory of Dan. An angel had appeared to Manoah's wife and told her that she would give birth to a son. The angel said, "Your son shall begin to save Israel from the Philistines. His hair must never be cut, for he will be dedicated to the service of God."

God blessed Samson with great physical strength, and as long as he did not cut his hair, his strength remained. However, he was not strong in character. He could be selfish, reckless, and mean. He often found himself in difficult situations of his own making. Even so, God used Samson to kill many Philistines, and because of this, the Philistines hated him.

Samson was courting a beautiful woman named Delilah, who was a Philistine. One day, some of her countrymen offered her money to betray Samson into their hands. So she convinced him to reveal the source of his strength to her. Samson told her that if his head was shaved, his strength would leave him. So Delilah lulled him to sleep and had all of his hair cut off. With his strength gone, Samson was captured by Philistine soldiers. They blinded him and threw him in prison, then they planned a great party to celebrate their victory. By the time the party took place, Samson's hair had begun to grow again. The Philistines brought him out of prison to mock him, and Samson stood between the pillars that held up the temple.

There were around 3,000 men and women on the roof of the temple, and all the rulers of the Philistines were there. Samson prayed, "LORD, remember me. Please, God, strengthen me just once more and let me get revenge on the Philistines." Then he pushed on the pillars with all his strength, shouting, "Let me die with them!" Down came the temple, killing everyone, including Samson.

Samson was born with great potential, but his character was never shaped. Sadly, he was blind to his own faults long before he lost his eyesight. Nevertheless, God used him to punish the Philistines as He rescued Israel yet again.

Judges 13–16

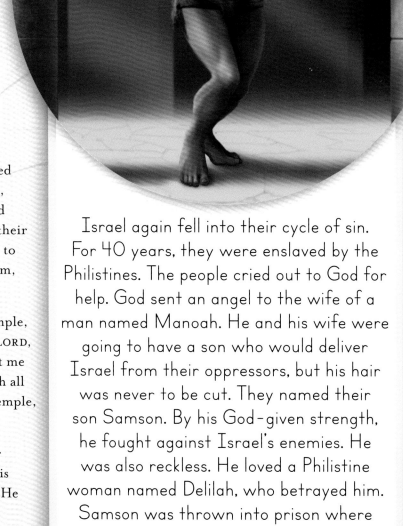

Israel again fell into their cycle of sin. For 40 years, they were enslaved by the Philistines. The people cried out to God for help. God sent an angel to the wife of a man named Manoah. He and his wife were going to have a son who would deliver Israel from their oppressors, but his hair was never to be cut. They named their son Samson. By his God-given strength, he fought against Israel's enemies. He was also reckless. He loved a Philistine woman named Delilah, who betrayed him. Samson was thrown into prison where he called out to God, and with his final breath, killed over 3,000 Philistines.

Ruth's Choice

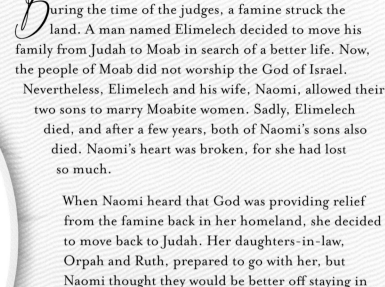

During the time of the judges, a famine struck the land. A man named Elimelech decided to move his family from Judah to Moab in search of a better life. Now, the people of Moab did not worship the God of Israel. Nevertheless, Elimelech and his wife, Naomi, allowed their two sons to marry Moabite women. Sadly, Elimelech died, and after a few years, both of Naomi's sons also died. Naomi's heart was broken, for she had lost so much.

When Naomi heard that God was providing relief from the famine back in her homeland, she decided to move back to Judah. Her daughters-in-law, Orpah and Ruth, prepared to go with her, but Naomi thought they would be better off staying in Moab. She was too old to remarry, but Orpah and Ruth were not. She loved them and wanted them to have every chance for happiness.

Orpah agreed to stay, but Ruth would not think of it. "Don't ask me to stay behind, for wherever you go, I will go. Your people will be my people, and your God will be my God. I will not leave you alone," she said.

Ruth was loyal and courageous. She had evidently come to understand that Naomi's God was the one true God. She was willing to leave behind everything she had ever known to follow this God, even if it meant moving to a strange and foreign land. What faith!

Ruth 1

As had happened to Jacob's family so long ago, a famine again hit the land of Canaan. A man named Elimelech moved his family to Moab to escape the suffering. Even though no one there worshiped the God of Israel, Elimelech and his wife, Naomi, let their sons marry women of Moab. As time passed, Elimelech and both their sons died. Their sons' widows, Orpah and Ruth, were told they could stay in Moab as Naomi planned to return to Judah. Ruth had come to know the one true God. She swore to stay with Naomi, even if it meant leaving behind the land and people she knew and loved.

Gleaning and Redeeming

Ruth and Naomi arrived in Judah, and Ruth began to glean grain in the field of a local farmer named Boaz. Gleaning was a practice included in the law (Leviticus 19: 9-10), where landowners left some grain behind during the harvest season so that the poor people of the community could harvest it.

Boaz was the son of Rahab, the woman who had helped Israel conquer Jericho many years before. He was a wealthy and honorable man. Boaz treated Ruth kindly and always made sure she and Naomi had enough to eat.

One day, he said to Ruth, "I've been told all about what you have done for your mother-in-law since the death of your husband — how you left your father and mother and your homeland and came to live with a people you did not know before. May the LORD repay you. May you be richly rewarded by the God of Israel, under whose wings you have come to take refuge."

Now, in those days when a man died, it was customary for one of his relatives to marry his widow and support her. The term for this was the "family redeemer." As it turned out, Boaz was one of Elimelech's relatives and was eligible to be a family redeemer. Naomi wondered — would God provide another husband for Ruth? Was it possible to have hope after all they had suffered?

Naomi told Ruth what she was thinking. Then she told her how to approach Boaz. Ruth followed her instructions to the letter, and sure enough, Boaz responded by offering to marry Ruth. The whole town celebrated. They were so happy for Ruth and also for Naomi.

Boaz and Ruth had a son and named him Obed. Then the local women said to Naomi, "Blessed be the LORD, who has not left you this day without a family redeemer. May his name become famous in Israel. He will renew your life and sustain you in your old age."

Naomi's faith was restored. Her sadness turned to joy. Not only did Ruth now have a husband who loved her, but Naomi had gained a son and a grandson! Obed would go on to become the grandfather of King David, whose descendants would include the promised Savior.

Ruth 1–4   Luke 3:32

Matthew 1:5

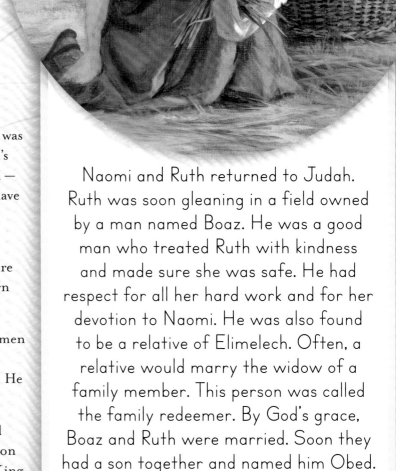

Naomi and Ruth returned to Judah. Ruth was soon gleaning in a field owned by a man named Boaz. He was a good man who treated Ruth with kindness and made sure she was safe. He had respect for all her hard work and for her devotion to Naomi. He was also found to be a relative of Elimelech. Often, a relative would marry the widow of a family member. This person was called the family redeemer. By God's grace, Boaz and Ruth were married. Soon they had a son together and named him Obed.

  The Last Judge

The Last Judge

One day a priest named Eli was sitting on his chair near the entrance of the tabernacle. A woman named Hannah had come to the courtyard to pray. Her prayers were full of emotion. Hannah explained to Eli that she was crying out to the LORD because she was unable to have a baby. Then Eli told her to go in peace and that God would grant her request. "If he blesses me with a son, I will dedicate him to the LORD's service," she promised.

Hannah soon discovered she was pregnant, and in time she had a son and named him Samuel. When he was weaned, Hannah took him back to Eli as she had promised.

Samuel served as Eli's personal assistant. He grew up to be an honorable young man who often heard the voice of the LORD. Now Eli had two sons of his own. They were priests like their father, but they were not honorable men. They had no respect for their father or for the LORD. God had warned Eli to correct his sons, but he had not done so. One night the LORD told Samuel that He was going to judge Eli and his sons because they had not obeyed Him. Not long afterward, the Philistines attacked Israel. They soundly defeated them and captured the Ark of the Covenant. Both of Eli's sons were killed in the battle. When Eli heard what had happened, he fell over in shock and died.

Samuel became the next, and last, judge of Israel. He convinced the people to stop worshiping idols and return wholeheartedly to the LORD. If they would do this, God would deliver them from the Philistines. Israel agreed. They gathered for battle at Mizpah, and Samuel prayed for them. The Philistines attacked, but this time God gave Israel the victory. The LORD protected Israel from the Philistines throughout Samuel's lifetime.

When Samuel was an old man, the people said to him, "Give us a king, just like the other nations have." Samuel was not happy with their request, but the LORD told him:

"Obey the voice of the people in all that they say to you, for they have not rejected you, but they have rejected me from being king over them. According to all the deeds that they have done, from the day I brought them up out of Egypt even to this day, forsaking me and serving other gods, so they are also doing to you. Now then, obey their voice; only you shall solemnly warn them and show them the ways of the king who shall reign over them" (1 Samuel 8:7–9).

> 1 Samuel 1–4, 7–9

Hannah was a woman of Israel who longed to have a child. She came to the tabernacle, crying and praying for this miracle. A priest named Eli heard her calling on God. When he found out what she was praying for, he told her that God would grant her request. Hannah eventually had a baby boy named Samuel. When he was old enough, Samuel began serving Eli. On one dreadful day, because of their disobedience to God, Eli and his two sons died. Samuel became the last judge for God's people. The nation would ask for a king. Though Samuel was not happy with this, God told him the people would have what they desired.

Israel's First King

Israel's First King

God was already Israel's true King, and He had proven over and over that He was a faithful King, one who truly cared about His people. Had the Israelites trusted Him, they would have lived very different lives. They would not have wanted another king.

Samuel warned Israel that a human king might demand much more from them than they realized. He would have the power to take their crops, their property, their freedom, and even their children. Samuel understood that power in the hands of a sinful man could do more harm than good. The people still demanded a king. So, God gave them what they asked for.

Samuel appointed Saul, the son of Kish, from the tribe of Benjamin to be Israel's first king. He was very tall, very handsome, and very rich. Saul was 30 years old when he was crowned. At first, he listened to Samuel. He led the Israelite army in many victories against their enemies. He showed great promise and was extremely popular with the people, but he cared more about pleasing people than he cared about pleasing God. On many occasions, he disregarded Samuel's advice and the LORD's commands.

One time, Saul and his army were preparing to go to war with the Philistines and realized they were outmatched. Saul had been waiting to engage in the battle because Samuel was on his way to offer a sacrifice to the LORD on their behalf. Saul's men were losing courage, so he took matters into his own hands and offered the sacrifice himself. Saul was not a priest, and offering sacrifices was not his job. Besides, he did not do it to honor God or to seek His help in the battle. He did it because he was impatient and did not trust God's timing.

When Samuel arrived and realized what had happened, he confronted Saul. "You have been foolish and have not kept the command of God. Had you obeyed Him, He would have established your kingdom forever. Since you did not, the LORD has rejected you as king."

Samuel turned to go, saying, "The LORD has torn the kingdom of Israel from you today and has given it to one of your neighbors — to one better than you. He who is the Glory of Israel does not lie or change His mind; for He is not a human being, that He should change his mind."

Samuel had tried his best with Saul. He had counseled him, supported him, and prayed for him for many years, but no more. He would mourn Saul, but he would not see him again. The LORD regretted that He had made Saul king.

1 Samuel 8, 9:1–2, 13–15

God was meant to be Israel's King, the one who would lead them and protect them. Instead, the people of Israel wanted a human king. Samuel tried to warn them that a king might demand everything from them. Even so, God gave them what they wanted. Samuel anointed Saul of the tribe of Benjamin to be their first king. Saul followed the wisdom of Samuel for a time, and so God helped the Israelites defeat their enemies. Saul, however, was filled with pride and soon only cared about what he wanted. Finally, Samuel let him know that God had rejected him. He would be king no more.

The Giant Slayer

The Giant Slayer

One day the LORD said to Samuel, "It's time to anoint a new king. Take the anointing oil and go to see Jesse of Bethlehem. I have chosen one of his sons to be king."

Samuel traveled to Bethlehem to meet Jesse, who was the grandson of Ruth and Boaz. Jesse had eight sons. When Samuel saw the oldest son, Eliab, he thought surely this is the LORD's anointed! Then the LORD said to Samuel, "Do not consider his appearance or his height; he is not the one I have chosen. I do not look at the outside of a person but at their heart."

One by one, Samuel met Jesse's other sons, who were all strong men and soldiers in Israel's army. Yet the LORD did not choose any of them. Finally, Samuel met the youngest son, David, who was a mere shepherd. He was the least likely choice. However, the LORD said, "This is the one, anoint him." So, he anointed the young man, and the spirit of the LORD was with David from that day forward, but it would be many years before he became king.

Samuel came to a man named Jesse, a grandson of Ruth and Boaz. He was told by God to anoint one of Jesse's sons as the new king. Though Jesse had eight sons, many of whom served in Israel's army, God chose the youngest, a mere shepherd named David. At that time, the Philistine armies came against the army of Israel. Goliath was a giant of a man in the Philistine army. Only David had the courage to face him on the battlefield. Though Goliath mocked David, this young man of Israel knew that God was with him. The giant came for him, but David struck him down with a single stone.

One day King Saul gathered his army to fight against the Philistines. The armies faced each other in a field near the valley of Elah. Goliath, a Philistine soldier, challenged Israel to send a soldier out to fight him one-on-one. "If you win, we will become your slaves. If I win, you will become ours!" he said.

Israel had a problem, a very big problem. Goliath was a giant of a man, standing over nine feet tall! His armor alone weighed around 125 pounds, and the head of his spear weighed 15 pounds. There was not a man in Israel's army with the courage to fight him. So for 40 days, Goliath strutted in front of Israel, taunting them.

David went to the soldiers' camp and saw how Goliath mocked Israel's army. He asked, "Who is this Philistine that he should defy the armies of the living God?" Then David offered to fight him. Saul replied, "There is no possible way you can win this fight." David persisted, and Saul finally agreed. He dressed David in his own armor and put a bronze helmet on his head, but the armor was too heavy, so David took it off. Then he went out to meet Goliath with nothing but his sling and five smooth stones.

Naturally, Goliath mocked David. Then David said, "You come against me with a dagger, spear, and sword, but I come against you in the name of Yahweh, the God of Israel's armies. It is Him you have insulted. Today, He will hand you over to me — and all the world will know that Israel has a God. It is not by sword or spear that the LORD saves, but by His power!"

Goliath stepped forward to attack, but David ran toward him. David shot a single stone from his sling and hit Goliath in the forehead. Goliath fell face down on the ground and then died. The Philistines ran when they saw that Goliath was dead, but the Israelites chased after them and killed them.

1 Samuel 16—17

Thread of Hope

God had chosen Israel to be a kingdom of priests and a holy nation. They were meant to point others to the one true God — to be an example of a different way to live. First they would need to learn who their God was and be willing to trust Him.

In a beautiful twist in the story, God used a woman named Rahab to illustrate what true faith looks like. Rahab was a Canaanite woman — an "enemy" of Israel. After hearing how Israel had been rescued by their God, she came to the conclusion that the gods of Canaan were worthless. She was willing to risk everything to come under the protection of the one true God.

With the help of Rahab and a rope dyed scarlet red, Joshua's spies escaped capture and execution. In return, Rahab and her family were spared when Israel returned and conquered Jericho. Her faith in God had saved her. It is interesting that this woman, who was not from Israel, placed her faith in God. Then she put her faith in action at great risk to herself. Rahab would later go on to marry a man from the tribe of Judah and become the mother of Boaz. Many generations later, she would be listed in the lineage of the promised Savior.

Under Joshua's leadership, Israel remained faithful to the Lord, although it did not take long for the people to fall into idol worship after Joshua died. God allowed them to suffer the consequences of their choices as He withdrew His protection from them. When the oppression from their enemies became too much to bear, the people cried out to God and He sent a judge to lead them. *Whenever the LORD raised up a judge over Israel, he was with that judge and rescued the people from their enemies throughout the judge's lifetime. For the LORD took pity on his people, who were burdened by oppression and suffering (Judges 2:18; NLT).*

As we have read, many of God's chosen people struggled to remain faithful to God. There were a few, like Ruth and Boaz, who did love and obey the Lord, but most people were like reeds swaying in the wind — following God one day and chasing after idols the next. Even so, God rescued Israel many times. You would think they would have learned to trust Him, but that is not what happened. The cycle of sin, consequences, repentance, and deliverance would be repeated many times over in Israel's history.

After the time of the judges ended, Israel entered into a new period. God's people had rejected Him as King so many times that He finally gave them what they asked for. They would have many human kings over the next several hundred years. God knew what the future would hold and the lessons that could be learned by living under the reign of both good and evil men. Sadly, there would be many dark days ahead as the Israelites continued to do what was right in their own eyes.

Throughout this last section, we have seen several clear examples of the blessings that came from placing one's faith in God and the consequences that came from refusing to. Yet God is merciful. Yes, He punishes sin. He will also forgive and restore when people repent. It is always the goodness of God and not the goodness of man that wins the day.

re·pent	to be truly sorry, to change course
for·give	to let go of anger, to not require payment or punishment
re·store	to return something or someone to an earlier and better condition

A Lasting Dynasty

As time went on, David became a mighty warrior. Everyone could see that the LORD was with him. The people of Israel considered him a hero. Not only had he killed Goliath, he had also killed thousands of Philistines.

Saul's son Jonathan and David became the best of friends, and at first, Saul loved David also. Over time, he became jealous because David was becoming increasingly popular with the people. He was afraid the people would want to make David their king. So he tried to kill him many times.

With Jonathan's help, David escaped from Saul. He and his men often hid among rocks or in caves, and even lived among the Philistines for a time. David had several chances to kill Saul during these years, but he refused to do so. He knew that he would take Saul's place one day, but he trusted that the LORD would bring that about at the right time.

Saul was eventually killed in battle, and the tribe of Judah anointed David as their king.

Saul's son Ishbosheth was proclaimed king over the rest of Israel. There would be many battles in the years ahead between those loyal to Saul's son and those loyal to David. As the years passed, David became stronger and stronger and Ishbosheth became weaker. After Ishbosheth's death, David was crowned king over all 12 tribes.

One day, Nathan the prophet told David, "The LORD declares that he will establish a house for you: After you die, he will raise up your son to succeed you. He will build a house for the LORD, and God will establish the throne of his kingdom forever."

Then David went and sat before the LORD and said, "Who am I, O LORD, that you would give me a lasting dynasty?" He was humbled and praised the mighty name of God.

David would go on to unify and lead Israel for many more years. Under his leadership, the boundaries of Israel grew to include the land from Egypt to the Euphrates River. The LORD gave him victory wherever he went, and his fame spread throughout the land.

- 1 Samuel 17–31
- 2 Samuel 2–8
- 1 Chronicles 14:8–17

Although Saul was still the king, the Lord was no longer with him. As David won many battles, Saul became jealous, fearing that David would take his kingdom. Saul even tried to have David killed. Finally, the day came when Saul himself was killed in a battle with the Philistines. The tribe of Judah declared that David was now king, though others declared that Saul's son Ishbosheth should be the king. For many years, there was war within the nation. Then after Ishbosheth died, David was crowned king over all Israel. David was victorious over his enemies because he trusted in God.

As king of Israel, David became known as a man after God's own heart. He worshiped God and sought His wisdom and blessing through all he did in his life. Even so, he was not a perfect man. He would fall and fail God at times, though he always approached God with a repentant heart. During his time as king, David wrote many psalms found in the Bible. These are songs of praise to God. These songs show David's love for God and reveal many of his own personal fears and struggles in his relationship with the Lord.

GLORIOSA DICTA SVNT DE TE. CIVITAS DEI.

PSALM. 86.

A Man after God's Own Heart

David did what was just and right for his people, but he was not a perfect man. Of the many battles he faced, some were within himself. He wanted to follow the will of God, but he sometimes made bad choices in his personal life. David did not escape the consequences of his actions, yet his deep love and respect for God always led him to repentance. During his lifetime, he was a shepherd, musician, soldier, poet, and king. He is most often remembered as someone who truly loved God and remained loyal to Him.

David wrote 73 of the 150 psalms in the Bible. They are a collection of poems and songs that served to remind Israel of all their God had done for them and to encourage them to love and worship God alone. Psalm 103 clearly illustrates why David is called a man after God's own heart:

Bless the LORD, O my soul,
and all that is within me,
bless his holy name!
Bless the LORD, O my soul,
and forget not all his benefits,
who forgives all your iniquity,
who heals all your diseases,
who redeems your life from the pit,
who crowns you with steadfast love and mercy,
who satisfies you with good
so that your youth is renewed like the eagle's.
The LORD works righteousness
and justice for all who are oppressed.
He made known his ways to Moses,
his acts to the people of Israel.
The Lord is merciful and gracious,
slow to anger and abounding in steadfast love.
He will not always chide,
nor will he keep his anger forever.
He does not deal with us according to our sins,
nor repay us according to our iniquities.
For as high as the heavens are above the earth,
so great is his steadfast love toward those who fear him;
as far as the east is from the west,
so far does he remove our transgressions from us.

As a father shows compassion to his children,
so the LORD shows compassion to those who fear him.
For he knows our frame;
he remembers that we are dust.
As for man, his days are like grass;
he flourishes like a flower of the field;
for the wind passes over it, and it is gone,
and its place knows it no more.
But the steadfast love of the LORD is from everlasting to
everlasting on those who fear him,
and his righteousness to children's children,
to those who keep his covenant
and remember to do his commandments.
The LORD has established his throne in the heavens,
and his kingdom rules over all.
Bless the LORD, O you his angels,
you mighty ones who do his word,
obeying the voice of his word!
Bless the LORD, all his hosts,
his ministers, who do his will!
Bless the LORD, all his works,
in all places of his dominion.
Bless the LORD, O my soul!

— Psalm 103

— 1 Samuel 13:14

— Acts 13:22

Wisdom Is Better Than Gold

Wisdom Is Better than Gold

Shortly before he died, David chose his son Solomon to be the next king. One night, God came to Solomon in a dream, saying, "Solomon, ask me for whatever you want."

Solomon responded, "Lord, you have made me king in my father's place, but I am like a small child. I don't know how to rule this nation. Please give me the wisdom I need, and help me know the difference between right and wrong."

It pleased God that Solomon acknowledged his need for wisdom instead of personal wealth and honor. So God gave him what he asked for. He also blessed him with fame and fortune. Therefore, Solomon became known as the wisest and richest king that ever lived. Like his father, David, he was a strong leader who also had a soft side. Solomon wrote the books of Proverbs, Ecclesiastes, and Song of Solomon in the Bible.

He built cities and formed alliances with surrounding nations. His most famous building accomplishment was the completion of a permanent temple for God. It was made from cedar and stone, and filled with bronze, silver, and gold. It was a work of art that took seven years to complete. Like the tabernacle before it, the temple had an inner room called the Holy of Holies.

After the priests placed the Ark of the Covenant inside the Holy of Holies, a cloud filled the temple. The LORD's glory and presence was so strong that the priests were overcome and unable to perform their duties. Then Solomon praised the LORD and blessed the people of Israel during a celebration that lasted for several days. It was an amazing moment in Israel's history. The king and his people were safe, successful, and devoted to God.

Sadly, over time, Solomon began to trust his own wisdom instead of God's. He wanted to make his own decisions. He ended up marrying hundreds of women who persuaded him to look for happiness outside of God. He even built shrines for their idols. This made the LORD angry.

"Since this has been your practice and you have not kept my covenant and my statutes that I have commanded you, I will surely tear the kingdom from you and will give it to your servant. Yet for the sake of David your father I will not do it in your days, but I will tear it out of the hand of your son. However, I will not tear away all the kingdom, but I will give one tribe to your son, for the sake of David my servant and for the sake of Jerusalem that I have chosen" (1 Kings 11:11–13).

The proverbs Solomon wrote contain wise advice that anyone would do well to follow, but what the king learned from his own failure is his most important legacy. In the Book of Ecclesiastes, he wrote that he had tried to find happiness in every activity under the sun, only to discover it had all been meaningless. What truly matters, he said, is to *"Fear God and keep his commandments"* (Ecclesiastes 12:13).

> 1 Kings 2–3, 6–11

> Ecclesiastes 1–12

David's son Solomon would become the next king. God came to Solomon in a dream, asking what he might desire as the new king of Israel. Solomon responded that he desired wisdom to lead God's people. So, God promised Solomon wisdom, as well as wealth and honor. King Solomon wrote books, songs, and proverbs, and he built cities and formed alliances with the surrounding nations. Above all this, he had a permanent temple built for God. Yet even Solomon turned away from God for a time. In the end, he realized his mistake.

A Tale of Two Kingdoms

Solomon reigned over Israel for 40 years. His reign was prosperous, but he had placed heavy tax burdens on his people in order to fund his building projects and lavish lifestyle.

After Solomon died, his son Rehoboam became the next king. The people asked him to ease their tax burdens in exchange for their support. The royal advisors who had served Solomon told Rehoboam to agree to their request. If he did, the people would be loyal to him. Rehoboam did not take their advice. Instead, he wanted the people to fear him. He told Israel that he would be even harder on them than his father had been. This proved to be a terrible decision.

The ten northern tribes rebelled against Rehoboam and decided to form their own kingdom. They were led by a man named Jeroboam who had previously served under Solomon. The prophet Ahijah had told Jeroboam that he would one day rule over ten of Israel's tribes, and that is exactly what happened. Jeroboam became king over the northern ten tribes, which retained the name of Israel.

The southern tribes of Judah and Benjamin remained loyal to Rehoboam. The southern kingdom became known as Judah.

So just as God had told Solomon would happen, the kingdom was torn in two.

It was a sad state of affairs. The 12 tribes of Israel had escaped from Egypt as one united nation. Through one miracle after another, they had seen and experienced the power and goodness of God. They had been chosen by Him to bear witness that He is the one true God, and they entered a covenant with Him. Even so, they allowed their own desires to cloud their judgment to the point that they either disregarded or totally forgot their purpose and their promise.

> *1 Kings 11—14*

> *2 Chronicles 10—12*

After Solomon died, his son Rehoboam became king. However, the people had grown tired under Solomon's rule. He had taxed them heavily and made them work hard to accomplish his plans. They asked Rehoboam to help ease their stress and suffering. The new king wanted the people to fear him and promised to only be harder on them. Soon the nation would be divided. The ten northern tribes of Israel broke away, declaring a man named Jeroboam as their king. Rehoboam ruled the now much smaller nation that came to be known as Judah. These united tribes were united no more.

The Northern Kingdom of Israel

God divided the kingdom of Israel in response to Solomon's sin and offered Jeroboam an incredible promise through the prophet Ahijah. He said, "I will make you king over Israel and you can rule over all that your heart desires. If you walk in obedience to me and do what is right, as David did, I will be with you, and I will give you a lasting dynasty."

Jeroboam was afraid the northern tribes would want to return to Judah to worship at the LORD's temple. If they did, they might change their minds and decide to support Rehoboam instead of him. So he established religious centers in the northern territory. Instead of building temples for God, he made golden calves (idols) for the people to worship instead.

In hindsight, it is hard to imagine anyone doing what Jeroboam did. God had promised to be with him and to bless him. All he had to do was trust and honor God over himself, but he did not. Instead, he tried to maintain the power and position God had given him by leading Israel to practice idol worship. In so doing, he lost the blessing. His dynasty ended with the death of his son Nadab.

Every king that followed in the northern kingdom was considered evil, for they did not seek the LORD. It appears that as the king went, so did the people. God sent many good prophets who taught and encouraged them to return to God, but they refused. Their hearts were bent on rebellion.

In all, the northern kingdom had 20 different kings. The nation lasted a little over 200 years. The prophet Hosea preached to them for over 40 of those years. In all that time, he saw little, if any, response to his message. Sadly, these people would suffer the consequences of their idolatry. God finally allowed the Assyrians to conquer them in 722 B.C.

Even so, God loved them, and He promised to restore them one day. *"And I will betroth you to me forever. I will betroth you to me in righteousness and in justice, in steadfast love and in mercy. I will betroth you to me in faithfulness. And you shall know the LORD"* (Hosea 2:19–20).

A few Israelites escaped capture and stayed in the land, but most who survived the war were banished to Assyria. Meanwhile, foreigners were brought in to resettle the land of Israel. The Israelites who remained intermarried with them and adopted their way of life and religion. This region became known as Samaria and its residents as Samaritans.

1 Kings 1–22

2 Kings 1–25

1 Chronicles 5:26

The Southern Kingdom of Judah

Sadly, King Rehoboam completely abandoned the LORD within just a few years and began to worship the false gods of Canaan. He knew there would be battles ahead as he tried to regain control of all 12 tribes, so he fortified all the cities of Judah in preparation. However, the kingdom was never united again.

For a time Judah fared a little better than Israel. They had some kings who followed the LORD, allowing for periods of peace and prosperity. They also had their share of bad and evil kings too, and with them came the worship of idols and false gods.

During the reign of Manasseh, the scroll containing the Law of Moses was discarded, and the temple fell into disrepair. The scroll was discovered in future years when King Josiah ordered that the temple be repaired. The king tore his robes when the scroll was read to him. He knew that Judah had defied the words of the law and their covenant with God. They were in danger of suffering the same fate as the northern kingdom.

He called together the people of Judah and read the words of the law to them. Then he called for a time of national repentance. He renewed the covenant between God and His people, pledging to follow the LORD with all his heart and soul. The people of Judah promised to do the same, and for as long as Josiah lived, they kept their promise.

Every king who reigned after Josiah was evil. It was during these years that the prophets Jeremiah and Ezekiel preached. Both men correctly predicted the fall of Judah and tried to warn the people, but they would not return to the LORD.

So God allowed King Nebuchadnezzar of Babylon to attack them. Nebuchadnezzar destroyed the city of Jerusalem, including the temple of the LORD. He took captives to Babylon in three phases, completing the banishment in 586 B.C.

The LORD, the God of their fathers, sent persistently to them by his messengers, because he had compassion on his people and on his dwelling place. But they kept mocking the messengers of God, despising his words and scoffing at his prophets, until the wrath of the LORD rose against his people, until there was no remedy (2 Chronicles 36:15–16).

- *1 Kings 1–22*
- *2 Kings 1–25*
- *2 Chronicles 36*
- *Jeremiah 25:1–11*
- *Ezekiel 12*

Letter to the Exiles

Jeremiah began his ministry during the reign of King Josiah and continued through the fall of Jerusalem under King Zedekiah. Many times he tearfully pleaded with his people to repent of their idolatry and return to the LORD, but they didn't listen. He was a very unpopular prophet. He often faced threats on his life and imprisonment. Once he was left to die at the bottom of a well, but he survived.

Nevertheless, Jeremiah loved God and his people and continued to preach the truth despite personal danger. After Jerusalem's citizens were taken captive to Babylon, Jeremiah sent them a letter to encourage them that God still loved them and that there was hope for their future.

Thus says the LORD of hosts, the God of Israel, to all the exiles whom I have sent into exile from Jerusalem to Babylon: Build houses and live in them; plant gardens and eat their produce. Take wives and have sons and daughters; take wives for your sons, and give your daughters in marriage, that they may bear sons and daughters; multiply there, and do not decrease. But seek the welfare of the city where I have sent you into exile, and pray to the LORD on its behalf, for in its welfare you will find your welfare. For thus says the LORD of hosts, the God of Israel: Do not let your prophets and your diviners who are among you deceive you, and do not listen to the dreams that they dream, for it is a lie that they are prophesying to you in my name; I did not send them, declares the LORD.

For thus says the LORD: When seventy years are completed for Babylon, I will visit you, and I will fulfill to you my promise and bring you back to this place. For I know the plans I have for you, declares the LORD, plans for welfare and not for evil, to give you a future and a hope. Then you will call upon me and come and pray to me, and I will hear you. You will seek me and find me, when you seek me with all your heart. I will be found by you, declares the LORD, and I will restore your fortunes and gather you from all the nations and all the places where I have driven you, declares the LORD, and I will bring you back to the place from which I sent you into exile (Jeremiah 29:4–14).

Jeremiah 1–52

Jeremiah warned the people of Judah to stay true to God. Many times he pleaded with them. They chose to follow evil kings anyway. So God allowed Jerusalem to be destroyed. The people were made slaves and taken to Babylon. Even though they had rejected God, He did not abandon them. Through His prophet Jeremiah, God declared: "For I know the plans I have for you...plans for welfare and not for evil, to give you a future and a hope" (Jeremiah 29:11).

Thread of Hope

David understood that sin hurts the heart of the LORD, and he was overcome with grief when sin was found in his own heart. Because of his love for God, David's reign was blessed and Israel prospered under his leadership. The blessings continued through the reign of Solomon, who was a powerful and successful leader during Israel's "golden years."

Solomon started off strong, but Satan had identified a weakness in him and used it to tempt him. Solomon married over 700 women during his reign. Though God had given him so much, he began to follow the advice of his many wives instead of God.

God responded by dividing the kingdom after Solomon died. These kingdoms battled against neighboring nations, but they also fought one another, brother against brother. They were anything but a light to the world. To add insult to injury, the northern kingdom began to worship golden calves instead of the one true God.

During these years, God sent prophets to warn both kingdoms of the consequences of rebelling against Him. These prophets were often ignored, mistreated, or even killed for their message. Still, these men and women of God made a difference, for there were some who listened to their teaching.

God's desire had always been that His people would trust and obey Him. Even when they rebelled, He gave them opportunities to repent and return to Him. God was patient with them, but eventually He allowed their sin to run its rightful course.

These people knew that God had rescued their ancestors from slavery. They knew He had promised to bless them if they honored their covenant with Him. Yet they still rebelled. They ignored God's warnings and chased false gods and idols of their own making. They wanted to decide what was right and wrong for themselves. So, they found themselves enslaved again.

Thankfully, God is faithful even when people are not, and He would fulfill His promises. In one of the most often quoted Scriptures from the Bible, He spoke words of hope to His captive people through the prophet Jeremiah.

"For I know the plans I have for you, declares the LORD, plans for welfare and not for evil, to give you a future and a hope" (Jeremiah 29:11).

They would not be slaves forever. Perhaps in losing everything, they would finally gain a heart for God.

proph·et	one who proclaims a message given to him or her by God
dy·nas·ty	a series of rulers from the same family
ban·ish	to be forced to leave one's country
wis·dom	an understanding of what is true and good, especially as to the ways of God

Dreams in Babylon

While slavery in Babylon was not what the survivors of Judah wanted, things could have been worse. They had been humbled, but at least they were alive. Jeremiah told them to settle in, for they would be in Babylon for 70 years. "Plant gardens and have families. Pray for Babylon, for in its welfare you will find your own," he said. So, that is what they did.

During this time, King Nebuchadnezzar of Babylon chose some young men from Judah's royal family to serve in his government. One of these men was named Daniel. He was among the wisest of all the king's students, and he faithfully followed God.

One night, the king had a dream that bothered him. He called for his wise men and demanded they tell him what the dream meant. "We would be happy to once the king tells us what he has dreamed," they replied. This made the king angry. He thought if they were truly wise, they would know what he had dreamed. So he sentenced all the wise men in his kingdom to die, including Daniel.

When Daniel learned what had happened, he went to the king and asked him to delay the executions so that he could inquire of the LORD. The king agreed, and Daniel asked some fellow Israelites to pray with him. During the night, the LORD revealed the king's dream and its meaning to Daniel.

The next day, Daniel told the king his dream had been of a large statue, made of gold, silver, bronze, and iron, with feet of clay. He explained that the statue represented the king's empire, along with the empires that would follow. "These empires will all fall at their appointed time," Daniel said. "But one day, God will send a kingdom that will last forever."

Then the king fell on his face. "It is true — your God is a revealer of mysteries. He is God of gods and LORD of kings!" Then he called off the executions, and Daniel became his most trusted official.

꙳ *Jeremiah 25:11, 29*

꙳ *Daniel 1—2*

Jeremiah the prophet told the people of Judah that they would be in Babylon as captives for 70 years. They were told to build homes, plant gardens, and pray for their captors. King Nebuchadnezzar of Babylon chose some of the royal captives of Judah to serve in his government. After having a disturbing dream, he asked his wise men to both tell him his dream and what it meant. None could do this, except for Daniel, who prayed to God for wisdom. Daniel knew the dream showed a statue of the king's rule and the kingdoms to come. The king then knew that the God of Daniel was above all gods.

One Hot Fire

Sometime later, King Nebuchadnezzar built a large statue of gold and set it up in Babylon. Then he held a dedication ceremony and invited people from all over his kingdom to attend. He told them they must bow down and worship the statue. Anyone who refused would be thrown into a fiery furnace. So, everyone did exactly as they were told. Well, almost everyone.

Three of Daniel's friends were at the ceremony. Shadrach, Meshach, and Abednego were Israelites who worshiped God and followed His law — the law that said, "You must not bow down before any other god." So they remained standing when everyone else fell to the ground.

The king was furious. He was not used to people defying him. He ordered that the furnace be heated seven times hotter than it normally was. Then he sentenced the men to death by fire. "Who do you think will rescue you from my hands?" he said to them. "Our God is able to deliver us," they responded. "But even if he does not, we will not worship this golden statue."

So the king's soldiers grabbed the men and tied them up. Then they hurled them into the furnace. The fire was burning so hot that it actually killed the soldiers who threw the men in, but Shadrach, Meshach, and Abednego were not harmed. The king was astonished. "Wait!" he said. "I see four men untied and walking around inside the fire, and the fourth man looks like a son of the gods! Shadrach, Meshach, and Abednego — come out at once."

Daniel's friends walked through the flames and stood before the king. Not one hair on their heads had been burned. They didn't even smell like smoke. "Blessed be your God, who sent his angel to deliver you. Therefore, I decree that anyone who speaks against the God of Israel will be executed. No other God can deliver his servants in this way."

What a testimony. These men would rather die than worship a false god. Because of their faith, everyone who was at that ceremony witnessed the power of the one true God.

Daniel 3

As time passed, King Nebuchadnezzar had a large statue of gold set up in Babylon. He wanted everyone in the city to come and bow down and worship the statue. Daniel's friends Shadrach, Meshach, and Abednego came to the dedication. They would not bow down, even when the king said that anyone not bowing would be thrown in a furnace of fire. The king was angry. He had the furnace made hotter than normal, ordering that the young men be thrown in, but they were not burned. Also, the king saw a fourth man in the fire with them. The king then blessed the God of Shadrach, Meshach, and Abednego who saved them.

The Lions' Den

Many years later, there was a new king in Babylon named Darius the Mede. He was so impressed with Daniel that he was thinking of promoting him to the highest office in the land. This made the king's other officials jealous. They wanted Daniel gone. They tried many times to catch him doing something wrong so they could accuse him before the king. Daniel was a righteous man and they were not successful. So they devised a plan to get him in trouble for doing something good instead. They convinced the king to make a new law that stated, "Whoever prays to any god, other than the king, must be thrown into a den of hungry lions."

Now, Daniel knew about the new law, but he continued to pray to the one true God, just as he had always done. Of course, the wicked officials reported him. The king realized he had made a mistake in passing the law. He tried to figure out a way to save Daniel, however, in those days a law signed by the king could not be undone. It was a clever plan indeed.

So Daniel was sentenced to the lions' den. Before they took him away, the king said, "May your God, whom you trust, deliver you!" The king spent the entire night fasting and praying for Daniel's safety. At first light, he ran to the lions' den. To his great relief, he found his friend alive and well. Daniel said, "The lions have not harmed me, O king, My God protected me because I am blameless before Him and you."

Then the king sentenced his wicked officials to the same fate they had arranged for Daniel. Unlike Daniel, they did not make it out of the lions' den alive.

That day, the king sent this message throughout his kingdom:

"Peace be multiplied to you. I make a decree, that in all my royal dominion people are to tremble and fear before the God of Daniel, for he is the living God, enduring forever; his kingdom shall never be destroyed, and his dominion shall be to the end. He delivers and rescues; he works signs and wonders in heaven and on earth, he who has saved Daniel from the power of the lions" (Daniel 6:25–27).

Daniel 6

Darius the Mede rose as the new king over Babylon. He came to honor Daniel above all the other officials, but they became jealous. They wanted to get rid of Daniel, but he never did anything wrong. So, they planned to bring him down through his devotion to God. They went to the king and had him sign a law that no one could pray to any god but the king. If they did, they would be thrown into a den of lions. Yet Daniel still prayed. Though he was tossed to the lions, the king prayed for his safety. In the morning, Daniel was found safe. The king made a new decree that all must worship Daniel's God, the one true God.

Homeward Bound

In 539 B.C., the Babylonian Empire was conquered by King Cyrus of Persia. Then the LORD placed it on the king's heart to rebuild the temple in Jerusalem. This fulfilled a prophecy spoken by Isaiah more than 100 years before.

"Who confirms the word of his servant and fulfills the counsel of his messengers, who says of Jerusalem, 'She shall be inhabited,' and of the cities of Judah, 'They shall be built, and I will raise up their ruins'; who says to the deep, 'Be dry; I will dry up your rivers'; who says of Cyrus, 'He is my shepherd, and he shall fulfill all my purpose'; saying of Jerusalem, 'She shall be built,' and of the temple, 'Your foundation shall be laid'" (Isaiah 44:26–28).

Cyrus issued a statement that said, "Thus says Cyrus, King of Persia, the God of heaven has told me to build a temple for him in Jerusalem. The Israelites who live in my kingdom are free to return to Judah to participate in this project. May your God go with you."

Now, not all of the Israelites wanted to return to Judah. It would be a long and difficult journey, especially for the elderly and those with small children, and many people now considered Babylon their home. Those who stayed behind helped by donating money and other resources for the project. The king even sent along the sacred items that had been stolen from the temple by King Nebuchadnezzar.

Around 50,000 Israelites made the journey. They took along 736 horses, 245 mules, 435 camels, and 6,720 donkeys. After they arrived and made homes for themselves, they rebuilt the altar of God. Then, according to the law of Moses, they made sacrifices to the LORD. Two years later, they began rebuilding the temple itself. The project continued through the reigns of Darius, Artaxerxes, and Xerxes, kings of Persia. The Israelites were met with opposition from their enemies many times during the construction, but God was with them.

When King Xerxes came to power, he sent Ezra to check on the progress. "Take whatever you need from my kingdom to restore the worship of your God in Jerusalem," he said.

When Ezra arrived, he found that many of the exiles had intermarried with surrounding people who worshiped false gods. Even some of the priests had rebelled against God in this way. Ezra fell to his knees and prayed for mercy. He was shocked that God's people had already turned their backs on Him. As the people heard Ezra lament and pray, they were convicted of their sin. Ezra challenged them to repent and return to the LORD. And most of them did.

2 Chronicles 36:22–23

Ezra 1–10

Nehemiah 1–13

Babylon was eventually conquered by King Cyrus of Persia. Then God put it on the king's heart to rebuild the temple in Jerusalem. Around 50,000 Israelites took the dangerous journey to Jerusalem to rebuild the temple. They would face many hardships and do the work of rebuilding for many years to come. So much time passed that a new king, Xerxes, sent a man named Ezra to see how everything was progressing. Ezra found that many were not following God, so he taught them, and they renewed their covenant with the LORD. The temple was finally completed under yet another king named Artaxerxes.

From Queen to Castaway

The Persian Empire was huge. By the time King Ahasuerus, also known as Xerxes, came to power, it consisted of 127 countries from India all the way to Ethiopia. In the third year of his reign, the king decided to invite all of his princes, military leaders, and noblemen to the capital city of Susa. He wanted them to see and admire all of the royal treasures.

The king held a grand banquet. This was no ordinary banquet, for nothing the king did was ordinary. He spared no expense for his guests. They gathered in the king's courtyard, which had been beautifully decorated. They ate the finest foods and enjoyed the best entertainment.

King Xerxes' wife, Vashti, did not attend the king's banquet. As queen, she was hosting her own banquet for the women of the royal court. On the seventh day of the king's feast, he sent seven of his servants to get her. He had put the glory of his kingdom on display but had saved the best for last. He wanted his guests to admire their beautiful queen.

The queen refused to come. The reason is not known, but she did not go when the king asked her to. Regardless of her reason, she must have known her refusal would be seen as an act of disrespect. The king was angry.

His royal advisors suggested he deal harshly with Vashti. They did not want anyone else to think it was okay to be disrespectful. Without respect, the kingdom would soon be overrun with troubles. So Vashti was stripped of her royal title and banished from the king's presence forever. She lost her title and her rights in a matter of moments.

No doubt Vashti regretted her decision, but some choices cannot be undone.

Esther 1

The vast Persian Empire of King Xerxes stretched from India to Ethiopia. In the third year of his reign, he called all his leaders to the city of Susa to look upon his treasures. The king had a celebration of his wealth for 180 days, then a great banquet for all his guests that lasted seven more days. On that last day of feasting, he had servants go and tell his wife, Queen Vashti, to come and show her beauty to his guests. She refused to come, and this angered the king deeply. The king's advisors told him to take away her royal title and banish her from his presence forever, and he did.

The Orphan Queen

Sometime later, the king's advisors suggested they search his kingdom to find a new queen — someone more worthy of the honor than Vashti had been. Representatives were sent far and wide to find the most beautiful young women in all the land and bring them to the palace in Susa. The king would choose a new queen from among them.

There were many Israelites (also known as Jews) who still lived in Persia at this time. Esther was a Jewish orphan who lived in the home of her cousin Mordecai. She was very beautiful and was taken to the palace with all the other women. Mordecai was like a father to Esther, and he warned her to tell no one her nationality. There were people who did not like the Jews, and he feared for her safety.

Of all the women brought to the palace, the king was most impressed with Esther. She was soon crowned queen of Persia. One day, Mordecai overheard a plot to kill the king. He reported it to Esther, who told King Xerxes right away. The king's life was spared that day because of their loyalty and quick thinking.

Sometime later, the king named Haman to be prime minister of the Persian Empire. Haman was a proud man who loved having people bow down to him. He also hated the Jews. Mordecai refused to show respect to this man, despite the palace officials pleading with him to do so. Haman was furious. When he learned that Mordecai was a Jew, he planned his revenge.

Haman convinced the king that the Jews in his kingdom were causing lots of problems. "They refuse to obey the laws of the king. If it please the king, issue a decree that they be destroyed, and I will donate 10,000 bags of silver to the king's treasury." The king believed Haman's lie and agreed to his request, and a date was set for the execution of every Jew in the Persian Empire.

>> *Esther 2–3*

King Xerxes decided to find a new queen. The most beautiful women of his kingdom were brought to him, and he chose Esther. Esther was a Jewish orphan who had been raised by her cousin Mordecai. Mordecai warned Esther not to tell the king that she was Jewish because there were some people in the kingdom who hated the Jews. One day, Mordecai discovered a plot to kill the king and reported it to Esther, and the king's life was saved.

Haman's Plan Backfires

News of the king's decree was sent all over the land, causing the Jews great distress. Mordecai dressed in burlap and ashes, the clothes of mourning, and cried bitterly. He sent word to Esther about what Haman had done. He asked her to go to the king and ask for mercy for her people. He said, "Perhaps you were made queen for this very purpose."

Esther told Mordecai to gather all the Jews in Susa and have them fast for three days. After the fast, she would approach the king. She must have been afraid, for the king did not know she was a Jew. In those days, it was against the law for anyone to approach the king without being invited. It was a crime punishable by death. Esther went anyway. She was willing to offer her own life to save her people if need be.

On the third day of the fast, Esther stood in the inner court of the palace. She was close enough to the throne room that the king could see her. When he did, he received her warmly. "Tell me why you have come. I will give you whatever you desire, up to half of my kingdom." Esther did not tell him what she wanted. Instead, she invited the king and Haman to a special banquet. Haman was so pleased — to dine at the queen's request was a great honor.

Haman's good mood didn't last. As he was headed home that day, he saw Mordecai sitting by the palace gate. Haman was filled with hatred and ordered that a gallows be built. He intended to hang Mordecai on it.

The following day, at the queen's banquet, the king asked, "Why have you invited us to this banquet? What is your request? I will grant it, even if it is half of my kingdom."

Queen Esther replied, "If it pleases the king, please spare my life and the lives of my people, for there is someone who wants to wipe us from the face of the earth!"

"Who would dare to harm the queen?" the king asked. Esther pointed to Haman and said, "It is the prime minister!"

It was then that the king and Haman both realized that the queen was Jewish. Haman grew pale with fear, and the king was beside himself with anger. Haman had manipulated him and plotted to kill his wife!

Then the king learned that a gallows had been built to hang Mordecai, a man who had saved the king's life. "Hang Haman on the gallows he built!" he ordered. So the plan to destroy the Jews was thwarted, and Haman was caught in his own trap.

Esther 4—7

Haman was an official in the king's court, and he hated the Jews. One day, he convinced the king that all the Jews in the kingdom should be killed. When Mordecai found out, he asked Queen Esther to help. She told Mordecai to have all the Jews in the city fast for three days, and after that she would approach the king. After the fast, Esther invited the king and Haman to a banquet where she revealed Haman's wicked plan to destroy her people. Now Haman would die instead.

Nehemiah's Prayer

Nehemiah was a Jewish man and a servant of King Artaxerxes. One day he learned that his countrymen in Jerusalem were in grave danger. The temple in Jerusalem had been repaired for some time, but the walls and gates of the city were in bad condition. This left the citizens vulnerable to attack from their enemies. So Nehemiah began to pray.

His words provide an excellent outline for any prayer:

» Adoration

» Confession

» Petition

"O LORD, God of heaven, the great and awesome God who keeps his covenant of unfailing love with those who love him and obey his commands, listen to my prayer! Look down and see me praying night and day for your people Israel. I confess that we have sinned against you. Yes, even my own family and I have sinned! We have sinned terribly by not obeying the commands, decrees, and regulations that you gave us through your servant Moses.

"Please remember what you told your servant Moses: 'If you are unfaithful to me, I will scatter you among the nations. But if you return to me and obey my commands and live by them, then even if you are exiled to the ends of the earth, I will bring you back to the place I have chosen for my name to be honored.'

"The people you rescued by your great power and strong hand are your servants. O Lord, please hear my prayer! Listen to the prayers of those of us who delight in honoring you. Please grant me success today by making the king favorable to me. Put it into his heart to be kind to me" (Nehemiah 1:5–11; NLT).

After praying, Nehemiah asked the king for permission to return to Jerusalem to rebuild the city walls, and the king agreed. So with God's help, Nehemiah and a team of men repaired the city walls in just 52 days. The people of Jerusalem were greatly encouraged and soon after renewed their covenant with the LORD.

» *Nehemiah 1– 7*

Nehemiah was a Jewish man who lived in Persia, serving King Artaxerxes. He found out that the people of Jerusalem were in danger because the city walls and gates were broken down. There was a great fear that they could be attacked by their enemies. So Nehemiah began to pray to God to help His people and to help the king show Nehemiah his favor. After praying, Nehemiah asked King Artaxerxes if he might return to Jerusalem to rebuild the city walls. The king agreed, and within just 52 days, the LORD helped Nehemiah and a group of men restore the walls of Jerusalem and their commitment to the LORD.

Malachi's Message

Sadly, rebuilding the temple and the walls of Jerusalem did not prove to be enough cause for God's people to stay true to Him. For it did not take long for them to break their promise again. They pretended to worship Him — but their hearts were far away.

Instead of giving God their best, they gave Him their worst. They brought animals to sacrifice that were sickly and lame. Their priests no longer taught the truth, and they allowed God's temple to fall into disrepair again. God was not pleased.

Throughout Israel's rebellious history, God had preserved a remnant of faithful people. We have read about many of them throughout this story. Noah, Abraham, Rahab, David, and Esther are just a few examples. They were not perfect, but they believed God and put their faith into action. They did their best to live for the LORD.

Most of the Israelites did not choose the same path. Malachi warned his generation about false worship and the coming judgment for those who practiced it, but most did not listen.

So, the LORD would offer His blessing and protection to people of other nations. *For from the rising of the sun to its setting my name will be great among the nations, and in every place incense will be offered to my name, and a pure offering. For my name will be great among the nations, says the LORD of hosts (Malachi 1:11).*

Thankfully, God provided a way for everyone to be saved. Malachi told about a day in the future when God Himself would come to save mankind from sin. First, He would send a messenger to prepare the way. Then He would come and redeem those who believe in Him. So that just as Noah, Abraham, Rahab, David, and Esther believed, so can we.

Behold, I send my messenger, and he will prepare the way before me. And the Lord whom you seek will suddenly come to his temple; and the messenger of the covenant in whom you delight, behold, he is coming, says the LORD of hosts (Malachi 3:1).

⁂ *Malachi 1–4*

Throughout Israel's history, God had always preserved a few people who were faithful to Him. These faithful few included Noah, Abraham, Rahab, David, and Esther. Even after the lessons learned from their captivity, most of God's people continued to wander away from Him. They pretended to worship God, they brought sickly animals to sacrifice, and the temple was falling apart. The prophet Malachi spoke of a time when God Himself would come to save everyone. Before this coming, a messenger would prepare the way for the Lord.

Thread of Hope

God is merciful and did not abandon His people when they were exiled. The stories of Daniel, Shadrach, Meshach, and Abednego prove that He was with His people in Babylon and that He was willing to face hungry lions and even walk through "the fire" of captivity with them.

Though I removed them far off among the nations, and though I scattered them among the countries, yet I have been a sanctuary to them for a while in the countries where they have gone (Ezekiel 11:16).

Israel's spiritual condition is clearly represented in the story of Vashti and Esther. Queen Vashti had the honor of being part of the royal family. She disrespected the king and was sent into exile. Likewise, Israel had the honor of being God's royal family. They disrespected their King (God) and were also sent into exile.

Vashti's banishment opened the door for Esther to become queen. God used Esther's humble obedience to preserve the Jewish nation and keep alive His promise that a Savior would come from the house of David one day, and also to illustrate that the outsider and the orphan are welcome in God's family.

These two queens represent the two paths we must all choose between. Vashti took her position for granted. She disrespected the king's command and did what she wanted instead, while Esther risked everything to save her people. In Esther's example, we see both the sacrifice and salvation of God, long before Christ was born.

In yet another act of God's mercy, He put it on the heart of a pagan king to restore the city of Jerusalem and the temple of God. Thousands of Israelites returned to Jerusalem to take part in the rebuilding. What an incredible turn of events! God had a plan and used enemy kings to bring it about. This did not happen because the Israelites were good, for they were most often rebellious. It happened because of God's goodness.

Even after all God had done for Israel, they still failed in their mission to be the example God had called them to be. Now, some might think that Satan was gaining ground here, but thankfully, none of this came as a surprise to God. He has allowed sin to continue so we can see the result of it with our own eyes. The world is broken because we have tried to rule it ourselves instead of submitting to God's rule.

God has always known what mankind needed. They needed a new heart (Ezekiel 11:19, 18:31, 36:26), and thousands of years of history have proven that He was right.

Thankfully, there is some VERY GOOD NEWS ahead. The Savior who was promised in the Garden of Eden would come, and He would accomplish what man had been unable to do.

ad·o·ra·tion	the act of worshiping
con·fes·sion	an admission of fault or sin
pe·ti·tion	a formal, important request

Table of Contents: Part Two ♡

Part Two:
A New Dawn

In Malachi's day, Jerusalem had been rebuilt, but the city was still under the control of the Persian Empire. In the years that followed, the land of Judea (Judah) came under the rule of Greece, Egypt, Syria, and Rome. All of these nations worshiped false gods and left their mark on Jewish culture. Many political and cultural changes had taken place.

As we pick up the story, it is around four hundred years after the temple in Jerusalem had been rebuilt. At this time in history, the Greek language and culture had spread throughout the known world. In addition, the Romans were building a paved highway system that would extend throughout the Roman Empire. These roads were used by citizens and soldiers and made travel much easier.

Judea was under the rule of Caesar Augustus, the emperor of Rome. Herod the Great served Augustus as the king of Judea. He was not popular with Jewish citizens for several reasons. One, he was not of the royal line of David. Two, he was a brutal leader whom the citizens feared, and finally, he ordered the people to pay unreasonably high taxes.

Israel had once been a unified and powerful kingdom under the reign of David, but those days were long gone. Now, they existed at the pleasure of the Roman Empire. Even though the Romans worshiped many false gods, the Jews were at least allowed religious freedom, and the temple continued to be the center of their rites and traditions. Nevertheless, they did not like being ruled by a government they feared. They wanted a new king — a Jewish king — the one the prophets had spoken of.

For to us a child is born,
to us a son is given;
and the government shall be upon his shoulder,
and his name shall be called
Wonderful Counselor, Mighty God,
Everlasting Father, Prince of Peace.
Of the increase of his government and of peace
there will be no end,
on the throne of David and over his kingdom,
to establish it and to uphold it
with justice and with righteousness
from this time forth and forevermore.
The zeal of the LORD of hosts will do this (Isaiah 9:6–7).

Dumbstruck

Zechariah was a priest who served in the temple of the Lord in Jerusalem. He and his wife, Elizabeth, loved the Lord and were careful to follow Him. They had always wanted a family of their own but had been unable to have children. Now they were quite old.

One day while Zechariah was in the temple, an angel appeared to him. "Do not be afraid," the angel said, "for God has heard your prayer. Elizabeth will have a son, and you are to name him John. He will be a man with the spirit and power of Elijah who will prepare the people for the coming of the Lord."

"We are too old to have a child. How can this be?" Zechariah asked.

"Because you have doubted my words, you will be unable to speak until the child is born. I am Gabriel, the Lord's messenger! It will happen just as I have said," the angel replied.

Sure enough, when Zechariah walked out of the temple, he was unable to speak. Soon afterward, Elizabeth became pregnant. It was a miracle! Zechariah and Elizabeth were so happy. Not only would they have a child, but the angel said he would be a man with the spirit of Elijah. It had been a long time since there had been a prophet like that in Israel.

Luke 1:5–25

Zechariah served as a priest in the Lord's temple in Jerusalem some 400 years after the prophet Malachi's message. Zechariah and his wife, Elizabeth, had wanted to have a child but had grown too old. One day, an angel appeared to Zechariah in the temple and told him that his wife would have a son who would be filled with the spirit and power of Elijah. Zechariah doubted how this might happen because they were so old, so the angel told him he would not be able to speak until their child was born. Soon Elizabeth was pregnant, just as the angel had said.

Another Birth Announcement

When Elizabeth was six months along in her pregnancy, the angel Gabriel was sent to Nazareth, a town in Galilee, to visit Elizabeth's cousin Mary. Mary was a descendant of King David. She was engaged to a man named Joseph, who was a carpenter. He was also a descendant of King David.

"Don't be afraid, Mary," Gabriel said, "for God is pleased with you. You will conceive and have a son, and you are to name him Jesus. He will be called the Son of the Most High. He will sit on the throne of his ancestor David and will reign over Israel forever. His Kingdom will never end!"

Mary was astonished. God had sent an angel to tell her she would give birth to the Messiah! Her people had been waiting so long for His arrival. Had the time finally come?

"How can this be?" she asked the angel. "For I have never been with a man."

The angel replied, "The Holy Spirit of God will make this happen. Your cousin Elizabeth is also going to have a child in her old age, for nothing is impossible with God."

"I am the Lord's willing servant. May His will be done," Mary said.

When Joseph found out Mary was expecting a child, he was upset. He did not yet understand she was carrying the Messiah in her womb. He was thinking of leaving her when an angel of the Lord appeared to him in a dream. "Do not be afraid, Joseph. The child Mary is carrying was conceived by the Holy Spirit. She will have a son, and you are to name Him Jesus, for He will save His people from their sins." Joseph believed and did as the angel said. He and Mary were soon married.

These things happened to make true what God had said through Isaiah, that a virgin would conceive and give birth to the Messiah.

» Isaiah 7:14

» Matthew 1:18–24

» Luke 1:32

» Luke 1:26–45

» Luke 3

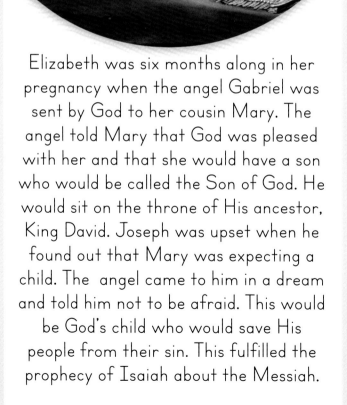

Elizabeth was six months along in her pregnancy when the angel Gabriel was sent by God to her cousin Mary. The angel told Mary that God was pleased with her and that she would have a son who would be called the Son of God. He would sit on the throne of His ancestor, King David. Joseph was upset when he found out that Mary was expecting a child. The angel came to him in a dream and told him not to be afraid. This would be God's child who would save His people from their sin. This fulfilled the prophecy of Isaiah about the Messiah.

A Prophet Is Born

The time came for Zechariah and Elizabeth's child to be born, and the whole town celebrated. The Lord had been so merciful to give them a son in their old age. Everyone expected them to name the child Zechariah, after his father. They were surprised when Elizabeth said, "No. His name will be John." They looked to Zechariah to see what he would say. Zechariah wrote on a tablet, "Yes, his name is John." Instantly, Zechariah could speak again. He was filled with the Holy Spirit and said,

Zechariah and Elizabeth's child was born, and all those who knew them were rejoicing. They expected that their new baby boy would be named after his father, but Elizabeth said they were going to call him John. All that were with them turned to Zechariah, and he wrote on a tablet, "His name is John." At that very moment, Zechariah could speak again. With his voice restored and his faith renewed, he began praising God and said, "Blessed be the Lord God of Israel, for he has visited and redeemed his people and has raised up a horn of salvation for us."

Blessed be the Lord God of Israel,
for he has visited and redeemed his people
and has raised up a horn of salvation for us
in the house of his servant David,
as he spoke by the mouth of his holy prophets from of old,
that we should be saved from our enemies
and from the hand of all who hate us;
to show the mercy promised to our fathers
and to remember his holy covenant,
the oath that he swore to our father Abraham, to grant us
that we, being delivered from the hand of our enemies,
might serve him without fear,
in holiness and righteousness before him all our days.
And you, child, will be called the prophet of the Most High;
for you will go before the Lord to prepare his ways,
to give knowledge of salvation to his people
in the forgiveness of their sins,
because of the tender mercy of our God,
whereby the sunrise shall visit us from on high
to give light to those who sit in darkness and in the shadow of death,
to guide our feet into the way of peace (Luke 1:68–79).

John grew into a spiritually mature young man. He lived in the wilderness until it was time for his ministry to begin.

Luke 1:57–80

The Messiah Is Born

Caesar Augustus ordered that a census be taken throughout the Roman Empire, so Joseph took Mary to his hometown of Bethlehem so they could be counted.

While they were there, the time came for her baby to be born. There were so many people in town for the census that they could not find a room to stay in. So Mary gave birth to Jesus in a humble stable. Then she wrapped Him in cloths and laid Him in a manger.

That same night an angel appeared to some shepherds who were guarding their flocks nearby. The men were terrified. "Do not fear," the angel said. "I bring good news! The Savior, the Messiah, the Lord has been born today! He is lying in a manger in Bethlehem." Then the angel was joined by the armies of heaven, who were praising God and singing, *Glory to God in highest heaven, and peace on earth to those with whom God is pleased. (Luke 2:14; NLT)*

The shepherds were amazed. "We must go to Bethlehem," they said. "We must see what the Lord has done!" Then they hurried to Bethlehem in hope of seeing the Christ child.

When they got there, they found things just as the angel had said. After they had seen the child, they told everyone they met what had happened. "The Messiah has been born in Bethlehem!" Then they headed back to their flocks, praising God as they went.

Luke 2:1–20

Caesar Augustus ordered that everyone in his realm be counted in a census. For this, all were forced to go to their hometowns to register. For Joseph and Mary, this meant traveling to Bethlehem. Even though Mary was pregnant, they made their way there but were unable to find any rooms available. Having to stay in a stable, Mary gave birth to Jesus and placed Him in a manger. An angel came to shepherds watching over their flocks to tell them of the Messiah's birth. The shepherds went as quickly as possible to find the Christ child, and they worshiped Him. Then they went home praising God.

A Special Child

Jewish law required that the firstborn son be dedicated to the Lord. So Joseph and Mary took Jesus to the temple in Jerusalem to present Him to God.

There was a righteous man named Simeon who lived in Jerusalem at the time. The Holy Spirit had revealed to him that he would see the Messiah before he died. He was at the temple when Joseph and Mary arrived with their baby.

Simeon took the child in his arms and said, "Oh Lord, I can now die in peace, for I have seen your salvation. The one you have prepared for all people and the glory of your people Israel! This child will cause many to rise and fall in Israel, and many people will speak against Him. The true nature of people will be revealed, and a sword will pierce your very soul." Mary and Joseph marveled at Simeon's words.

There was also a woman named Anna at the temple that day. She was an older woman whose husband had been dead for many years. Anna spent her time at the temple worshiping God and praying. She walked up as Simeon was talking with Mary and Joseph, and she began to praise God. Then she shared the good news about the child to everyone who had been waiting for God to rescue Jerusalem.

Luke 2:22–38

Joseph and Mary brought their new baby to the temple in Jerusalem to dedicate Him to God. A righteous man named Simeon was there, hoping to see the Messiah before he died. He lifted up the baby Jesus and said, "Oh, Lord, I can now die in peace, for I have seen your salvation." He let Jesus' parents know that their son would be the reason that many in Israel would rise up and a reason that many would fall. Also at the temple was a widow named Anna. She praised God for the child and shared the good news about His birth with others.

Wise Men Meet an Evil King

Now, there were some wise men in the east who had made their way to Jerusalem. They came to worship the child who had been born King of the Jews. They said they had seen His star when it rose and had traveled many miles to give honor to the new King. Herod the Great was disturbed when he heard what the men said. He was threatened by the possibility of a new king. Could this child be the one the Jews had been waiting for? He called together the chief priests and the teachers of the law and asked them where the Messiah was supposed to be born. "In Bethlehem," they told him.

So, the king tried to trick the wise men into helping him find the child. "Go to Bethlehem and search for the child. Let me know as soon as you find Him," he said. "Then I will go and worship Him also." Herod secretly planned to have the child killed.

The wise men set out for Bethlehem and were thrilled to see that the star appeared again and led them right to the child. They found Him in a house with His mother, and they bowed before Him and gave Him gifts of gold, frankincense, and myrrh. Then they left the area without returning to Herod.

Soon after, an angel appeared to Joseph and warned him to take Mary and their son and flee to Egypt. "Stay there until I tell you it is safe to return. For Herod the Great will try to kill Him," he said. So, Joseph left with his family in the middle of the night.

The king was furious when he learned that the wise men had left without telling him where the boy was. Because he did not know which child was the supposed new king, he ordered that all the boys in Bethlehem who were two years old or younger be killed.

Sometime later, Herod the Great died. His kingdom was then divided into four separate districts, each with its own ruler. Then an angel appeared to Joseph and told him it was safe to return to Israel. So, he moved his family back to Nazareth. Jesus was a strong and healthy child who grew in wisdom and favor with God and with everyone who knew Him.

Matthew 2:1–23

A group of wise men from the east came to Jerusalem, looking for the Messiah. They spoke to King Herod, hoping he might help them find this new ruler. Herod saw this new ruler as a threat to his kingdom and wanted to harm the child. So he tried to trick the wise men into helping him find the boy. A star's light guided the wise men to Jesus, and they gave Him gifts of gold, frankincense, and myrrh. Then they returned home without going back to Herod. Joseph also took his family and left for Egypt because an angel had told him that Herod wanted to kill the child. After Herod died, the family returned to the land of Israel.

  Preparing the Way

Preparing the Way

People had been wondering what would become of John since his unusual birth many years before. When he was 30 years old, he began to preach in Judea and became well-known in the area.

His father had served God in the temple, but John would serve God in the wilderness. Instead of the special garments a priest normally wore, John wore clothes woven from camel hair. Instead of enjoying the food set aside for the priests, he ate wild honey and locusts. He was unusual, to say the least. He had separated himself from normal Jewish religious practices in order to make a point — God cares about the heart of a person — not their outward appearance, or their heritage.

He traveled up and down both sides of the Jordan River, telling people that it was not enough to be a descendant of Abraham. They also needed to repent of their sins. Those who listened to him were baptized in the river, and John became known as "John the Baptist." Baptism was an outward sign that they were sorry for their sin, but it was only the first step. If they were truly sorry, they would change the way they lived. "How should we change?" the crowds asked.

John responded, "Be kind to the poor. Be fair and honest. Be content with what God provides."

Notice that John did not speak of following to the letter all of the Jewish laws that existed at the time. Instead, he spoke of a changed heart. Being kind, fair, honest, and content are matters of the heart. He knew that when a person's heart changes, their actions will follow. It was a similar message to what the prophet Micah had preached many years before (Micah 6:6–8).

Some people wondered if John was the Messiah, but he told them, "No, I am not worthy to even untie His sandals. Know that He is coming soon!"

One day, Jesus came down from Galilee and wanted John to baptize Him. Instead, John said, "You should be the one baptizing me!"

"We must do as God says," Jesus replied. So John baptized Him.

As Jesus came out of the water, the heavens were opened and the Holy Spirit of God came down like a dove and settled on Him. A voice from heaven was heard saying, "This is my beloved Son, who brings me great joy."

After he baptized Jesus, John continued to preach and call people to repentance. His message was unpopular with the king, so he was finally arrested and thrown into prison.

Matthew 3:1–16

Mark 1:1–11

Luke 3:1–22

Micah 6:8

Zechariah and Elizabeth's son, John, turned 30 years old and preached along the Jordan River. His message was of repentance, turning from your sins. Those who followed him and wanted to change from their old life were baptized in the river. Baptism, being placed under the water and lifted up, was an outward way to show that you had changed on the inside. Jesus came to John and asked to be baptized. John tried to refuse, but Jesus said that this must be done. When Jesus was lifted up, the Holy Spirit came down on Him like a dove, and a voice said, "This is my beloved Son, who brings me great joy."

Jesus Is Tested

After being baptized, Jesus was told by the Holy Spirit to pray and fast, and Satan tempted Him for 40 days. First, Satan tried to trick Jesus into turning stones into bread. Jesus replied with Scripture: "Man does not live by bread alone." Then Satan told Jesus he would give Him all the kingdoms of the world if He would bow down. Again, Jesus replied with Scripture: "You must worship the Lord your God only." Finally, Satan brought Jesus to the temple and said the angels would catch Him if He threw Himself down. Jesus again used Scripture to fight Satan: "Do not put the Lord your God to the test."

After He was baptized, the Holy Spirit led Jesus into the wilderness where He was tempted by the devil for 40 days. Sin, suffering, and death had plagued mankind ever since Adam had disobeyed God in the Garden. Satan's schemes and mankind's sinful nature had worked together to produce a very broken world. Satan knew who Jesus was and that He had come to save the world from sin. So he tempted Jesus with the same tactics he had used in the Garden.

Jesus was ready for him. Jesus knew He would need the power of the Holy Spirit to win this battle. He proved that the power of the Spirit is stronger than the power of the flesh. He was armed for battle with the Word of God.

Of course, Satan attacked where he thought Jesus was weakest. Knowing that Jesus had fasted and was hungry, he said, "Turn this stone into a loaf of bread if you are the Son of God." Jesus replied, "No! The Scriptures say that 'Man does not live by bread alone.' "

Next, he tempted Jesus with worldly power by offering to give Him all the kingdoms of the world. "I will give you authority over all of them — if you will worship me!" he said. Again, Jesus responded by quoting the Word of God. "The Scriptures say, "You must worship the Lord your God only!' "

Finally, Satan took Jesus to the highest point of the temple in Jerusalem. "Throw your self off! If you are truly the Son of God, he will send his angels to protect you."

Jesus answered, "Again, the Scriptures say, 'Do not put the Lord your God to the test." Jesus had come to do the will of God, and He would not let God's enemy sway Him. By the Word of God and the power of the Spirit, He was victorious over Satan. Then He commanded the devil to leave Him alone, and the devil obeyed Him.

Be gone, Satan! For it is written, "You shall worship the Lord your God and him only shall you serve" (Matthew 4:10).

- *Matthew 4:1–11*
- *Luke 4:1–12*
- *Mark 1:12–13*
- *Deuteronomy 6:13, 8:3, 10:20*

Thread of Hope

The decree of a Roman emperor had caused Mary and Joseph to go to Bethlehem to take part in a census. As it happened, Mary gave birth there. This fulfilled Micah's prophecy that the Messiah would be born in Bethlehem. It also illustrates that God is sovereign, even over rulers who do not believe in Him. Caesar Augustus had no idea his census was part of God's plan.

Jesus' birth was first revealed to humble shepherds. Not to Herod the Great or Caesar Augustus. Not to the religious leaders of Israel, but to ordinary men. These men experienced a glimpse into the heavenly realm as they saw and heard the angelic host rejoicing at the birth of Jesus. They were so moved that they left their flocks to find Him, and they worshiped Him.

Prophecies fulfilled on that most holy night.

> *But you, Bethlehem Ephrathah, though you are small among the clans of Judah, out of you will come for me one who will be ruler over Israel, whose origins are from of old, from ancient times (Micah 5:2; NIV).*

> *But you, Bethlehem, in the land of Judah, are by no means least among the rulers of Judah; for out of you will come a ruler who will shepherd my people Israel (Matthew 2:6; NIV).*

> *Does not Scripture say that the Messiah will come from David's descendants and from Bethlehem, the town where David lived? (John 7:42; NIV).*

Most people were completely unaware that a world-changing event had just happened.

Around 30 years later, John began to set the stage. Both Isaiah and Malachi had predicted his ministry and message hundreds of years before he was born (Isaiah 40:3; Malachi 3:1). John's purpose was to prepare Israel for the arrival of the Messiah. Now, the idea of the Messiah was not something new to the Jews, for He had been promised in the Scriptures. First, in Eden, and then to Abraham, Isaac, Jacob, and King David. They knew He was supposed to come someday. John the Baptist told them to get ready. "Repent! For the King is coming," he said.

Most Jews wanted to be a proud and strong nation again. They also had their own ideas of what the Messiah would be like. They were expecting a conquering warrior, one who would reclaim Israel from Rome by force.

They were not expecting the humble son of a carpenter.

cen·sus	an official counting of the people who live in a country or territory
Mes·si·ah	the Hebrew word for "chosen one"
sov·er·eign	a ruler with supreme power or authority
bap·tize	to immerse in water as a symbol of being cleansed of sin
re·pent	to be sorry for a sin, along with a desire not to repeat that sin

Fishing for Men

After He was tempted by Satan, Jesus went to live in Capernaum, a town on the Sea of Galilee. This fulfilled the prophecy of Isaiah, which said, *...but in the future he will honor Galilee of the nations, by the Way of the Sea, beyond the Jordan — The people walking in darkness have seen a great light (Isaiah 9:1–2; NIV).*

Jesus began His preaching ministry there. One day, He was walking beside the sea when He came upon some fishermen who were cleaning their nets. They were two sets of brothers: Andrew and Peter, and James and John.

Jesus got into Peter's boat and asked him to row out into the water and cast out his net. Peter replied, "We worked all night long and didn't catch a thing." Still, he did as Jesus asked and was amazed by what happened next. He caught so many fish that the net began to break apart. So James and John rowed out to help. It was the biggest catch they had ever seen, enough to fill both boats.

"Follow me," Jesus said, "and I will teach you to fish for people instead." All four men left their boats and followed Jesus.

- Matthew 4
- Mark 1
- Luke 5:1–11
- John 1

For a time, Jesus lived in Capernaum, near the Sea of Galilee. This fulfilled Isaiah's prophecy stating that in Galilee the people who had walked in darkness would see a great light (Isaiah 9:1–2). Soon, Jesus was teaching beside the sea. One day, He got into the boat of Peter and Andrew and told them to go out in the water and cast their nets. Peter told Jesus they had caught nothing all night, yet he did as Jesus asked. So many fish filled the nets that James and John came out to help. Then Jesus told all four men to follow Him and become fishers of men. They went with Him immediately.

A Wedding Miracle

The next day, Jesus and His followers left for Cana (a town in Galilee) to attend a wedding. Before they headed out, Jesus sought out Philip and said, "Follow me." Philip went to find his friend Nathanael (also known as Bartholomew). He found him sitting under a fig tree and said, "We have found the Messiah, the one Moses and the prophets spoke about. He is Jesus of Nazareth, the son of Joseph."

Nathanael replied, "Can anything good come from Nazareth?" Out of curiosity, he went with Philip anyway.

It did not take long for Nathanael to be convinced that Jesus was the Messiah. Jesus was waiting for him and told Nathanael that He had seen him sitting under the fig tree before Philip asked him to come. Jesus had been nowhere near that fig tree, and Nathanael knew it. Yet, Jesus had been aware of him.

"You will see greater things than this," Jesus told him. So Nathanael left everything behind and followed Jesus also.

Jesus and His followers headed to Cana. In those days, weddings lasted for several days and people traveled many miles to celebrate with the bride and groom. Jesus' mother and brothers were also at this wedding, and they were all enjoying the festivities together. Then the wine ran out in the middle of the celebration, and the groom's family was embarrassed. So Mary asked Jesus to help.

"My hour has not yet come," He said to her.

However, Mary told the servants, "Do whatever he tells you to do."

Jesus honored His mother's request. There were six empty stone jars nearby — ordinary vessels used to store water for washing hands. Jesus told the servants to fill the jars with water, and they did. When the servants went to draw water out of the vessels, they found that the water had turned to wine! It was the best wine they had ever tasted.

The master of ceremonies complimented the bridegroom. "Normally, people serve the best wine first and save the cheaper wine for later. You have done just the opposite. You have saved the best for last." He had no idea where this new wine had come from, but the servants knew. Mary and the disciples also knew.

This was the first time Jesus revealed His glory by proving that He had power over the material world.

John 1:43–51, 2:1–12

Matthew 13:55

Jesus and His followers attended a wedding in a town called Cana. Weddings during this time often lasted several days. All were enjoying the special occasion, but during the celebration, the wine for the wedding ran out. Mary, Jesus' mother, came to Him for help. He did not wish to reveal Himself yet, but she told the servants there to do whatever He asked them. He had them fill up six large stone jars with water. When they drew out some of the water, they found it had turned to wine. This was the first time Jesus revealed His miraculous power over nature.

 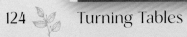 Turning Tables

Turning Tables

Passover was approaching, so Jesus and His disciples went to Jerusalem. People from all over Judea had also come to celebrate this annual event. Since everyone who visited the temple was required to pay a temple tax and make a sacrifice, the religious leaders had allowed merchants to set up shops inside the temple grounds. There were people selling animals for sacrifices and others who were charging fees to exchange foreign currency.

Jesus became angry when He saw this. The temple of God was meant to be a place of worship, not a place of business and personal profit. So He made a whip out of some rope and drove the animals out of the temple. He chased out the businessmen too, turning over their tables. He told them, "Stop turning my Father's house into a marketplace!"

Most of the religious leaders did not like Jesus because He had pointed out their hypocrisy and interfered with their money-making schemes. Nevertheless, Jesus performed many miracles on that trip to Jerusalem, and many people began to believe in Him.

Not all of the religious leaders felt that way, though. One of them sought Jesus out that night to speak with Him. His name was Nicodemus, and he was a teacher of the law. Unlike the other leaders, Nicodemus was trying to understand Jesus. "God must have sent you to us," he said, "for no one could perform these miraculous signs without God's help."

Jesus replied, "A person can't see the kingdom of God unless they are born again."

"How is that possible? Can an old man return to his mother's womb?" Nicodemus said.

"You are a Jewish teacher," Jesus replied. "Still you do not understand. I am talking about heavenly things. No one has ever gone up to heaven and then come back, but the Son of Man has come down from heaven, and everyone who believes in Him will have eternal life."

For God so loved the world that he gave his one and only Son, that whoever believes in him shall not perish but have eternal life. For God did not send his Son into the world to condemn the world, but to save the world through him (John 3:16–17; NIV).

When Jesus told Nicodemus he must be born again, He was talking about a spiritual birth. That birth happens when a person places their faith in Jesus as Lord and Savior. Not only will they have eternal life in heaven, but they will also experience spiritual aspects of God's kingdom on earth.

Nicodemus had a lot to think about. Would he choose to stay loyal to the old way of religion, or would he choose to believe that Jesus was the answer to the problem of sin?

John 2:13–24, 3:1–21   Matthew 5:17

Many during the Passover festival came to the temple, and those who did were required to pay a tax and make a sacrifice. The religious leaders allowed merchants to sell sacrificial animals inside the temple area, a place of prayer, and to charge people extra for services. This made Jesus angry, so He chased them from the temple. Nicodemus, a teacher of the law, came to Jesus at night, wanting to understand His message. Jesus told him that one could only enter heaven if born again and that God loved the world so much that He gave His only Son so people could be saved through Him.

Drink from this Well

Drink from this Well

Jesus decided to return to Galilee by way of Samaria. This territory had been taken by the Assyrians when they conquered the northern kingdom of Israel in 722 B.C. The land was inhabited by Israelites who had intermarried with the foreigners who had resettled the land after the Assyrian captivity. It was generally forbidden for Jews to intermarry with Gentiles for fear the Jews would adopt their idolatrous practices, and that is what happened. Though the Samaritans continued to worship the Lord, they had also worshiped idols (2 Kings 17:24-40). For this reason, the Jews in Judea would have nothing to do with them. Jesus made a point of stopping at a well in Samaria. His followers went to a nearby town to find something to eat, but Jesus stayed behind. Soon after, a Samaritan woman came to the well to draw some water.

"Please give me a drink," Jesus said to her. "Why ask me for a drink?" she said. "For you are a Jew and I am a Samaritan."

He replied, "If you knew who I truly am, you would ask me for water. For I have water to drink that is unlike anything you have ever tasted."

"This is a deep well," she said. "You don't even have a bucket to draw water. Besides, how could you offer better water than what comes from this well?" Jesus responded, "Whoever drinks from this well will be thirsty again within a short time. The water I offer becomes like a fresh spring inside them. It gives eternal life and never runs dry."

"I would love to never be thirsty again; please give me some of the water you speak of," she said.

Then Jesus told her to get her husband. When she told Him that she did not have a husband, He responded, "That's right! You are not married, but you have had five husbands. The man you are living with is not your husband."

The woman realized that this man must be a prophet. So she asked Him, "Why do you Jews believe that God must be worshiped in Jerusalem? We Samaritans believe it is all right to worship him here in our own land."

"You know little about the one you worship," Jesus said. "The time has come for all worshipers to worship the Father in spirit and in truth. The Father is looking for a people who will worship Him that way."

Then the woman said, "I may not know much, but I know the Messiah is coming — the one who is called Christ. He will teach us when He comes."

"I am the Messiah," Jesus said.

The disciples returned at that moment, and they were surprised to find Jesus talking to a woman, especially a Samaritan woman.

John 4:1–27

2 Kings 17:24-40

Coming home to Galilee, Jesus chose to pass through the region of Samaria. Though many of the Jews looked down on the Samaritans because they were a mixed race of Jews and Gentiles, Jesus sought out a Samaritan woman at a well. He asked her for some water, and she wondered why a Jewish man would ask anything of a Samaritan. Then He began to speak with her about her life in great detail. He knew she had been married five times and was now with a man who was not her husband. She knew He must be a prophet. Jesus revealed that He was the Messiah.

Many Samaritans Believe

Then the woman left the well and returned to her village, telling everyone, "Come and see this man at the well. He knew everything about me. Could He be the Messiah?"

Meanwhile, the disciples tried to get Jesus to eat the food they had brought. Then He said, "I am nourished by doing the will of God who sent Me. Look around you, the fields are ripe for harvest. God desires we bring in a harvest of people who will love and believe in Him. There will be much joy for those who plant and those who harvest, for those who believe will receive eternal life."

Many people from the village followed the woman back to the well. When they heard that Jesus knew about her past and had still offered her hope and good news, they wanted to see Him for themselves. Was this man really a prophet? Did He truly have good news that included the Samaritans? After meeting Jesus, they begged Him to stay in their village, and He did stay for a few more days — enough time for many more people to hear His message and believe. "He is the Savior of the world!" they exclaimed.

John 4:28–42

When the disciples found Jesus, they thought it strange that He would be talking with a Samaritan woman. She soon left and went to her village to tell everyone of Jesus. She let them know how Jesus had known everything about her and wanted her to find God's salvation. The woman even wondered if Jesus might be the promised Messiah. Soon, many people from the village came out to be with Jesus and asked Him to stay with them a little longer. He remained a few days, teaching them about the kingdom of God, and many more believed in Him.

Power and Authority

After spending a few days with the Samaritans, Jesus made His way to Galilee. He was filled with power from the Holy Spirit, and He taught in synagogues throughout the land. Reports about Him spread quickly, for He was able to drive out evil spirits and heal people of their diseases. He taught with such authority. He simply spoke and miraculous things happened. No one had ever seen anything like it.

One time while He was teaching in Capernaum, a man with an evil spirit cried out,

"Get out of here, Jesus of Nazareth! Why are you interfering with us? I know who you are, the Holy One from God."

"Come out of this man at once," Jesus said to the demon. As the crowd watched, it left the man. Everyone who saw this was amazed.

Another time, Jesus had gone to Simon Peter's home to visit. He arrived to find Peter's mother-in-law very sick with a fever. He rebuked the fever, and it left her. Then she got out of bed right away and prepared a meal for Jesus and His followers.

Soon people began to bring their sick friends and family members to Jesus to be healed. Then by the touch of His hand or the word of His mouth, they were.

As He traveled from town to town, word about Jesus spread.

- Mark 1:14–39
- Luke 4:14–44
- John 4:43–45

Jesus returned to Galilee, filled with the power of the Holy Spirit. He taught in the synagogues, drove out evil spirits, and healed the sick. A man in Capernaum who was possessed by an evil spirit cried out for Jesus to go away. The evil spirit recognized Jesus as the Holy One from God. Jesus spoke to the demon and told it to come out of the man, and it did. There was also a time when Peter's mother-in-law was sick, and Jesus rebuked the fever, and she became perfectly well. Soon, Jesus was going from town to town to teach and heal the sick.

Who Does He Think He Is?

One day, there was a long line of people waiting to be touched by Jesus, and a large crowd stood around to hear Him speak. There were some men who had brought a paralyzed friend to be healed, but they could not make their way through the crowd. So they climbed onto the roof of the house where Jesus was and removed the ceiling tiles. Then they lowered their friend through the roof and laid him down at Jesus' feet. When He saw the faith of these men, Jesus said to the man, "My friend, your sins are forgiven."

Now, there were some religious leaders in the crowd who were offended by this. They thought to themselves, "Who does this man think he is? Only God can forgive sins!"

However, Jesus knew what they were thinking. He said, "Your thoughts are not right, for the Son of Man has been given the authority to forgive sins. Do you think it is easier to say, 'Get up and walk,' than it is to say, 'Your sins are forgiven'?" Then Jesus proved to them that He had this authority. He told the man, "Stand up. Pick up your mat and go home." The man got up! He was so happy, and he praised God, and everyone who witnessed this miracle was filled with awe.

Another time, Jesus and His followers were walking through some fields of grain on the Sabbath (day of rest). They picked some of the ripe grain and ate it. Now, Jewish law did not allow people to work on the Sabbath, so some of the leaders asked Jesus why He allowed His followers to work by picking grain. Jesus answered by saying, "The Son of Man is lord of the Sabbath."

On another Sabbath, He healed a man whose hand was paralyzed. He knew what the religious leaders were thinking, and He said, "Is it better to do good or to do evil on the Sabbath?" The religious leaders were very upset because this man was a threat to their time-honored and rule-based religious system. The people were starting to follow Him.

So, they began to discuss ways to stop Him.

Luke 5:17–26, 6:1–11

The powerful ministry of Jesus brought out many people to see Him. Sometimes those who were sick could not get to Him in order to be healed. One time, some men brought a paralyzed friend to Jesus. Unable to reach Him, they cut a hole in the roof so they could lower their friend down. Jesus said to the man, "Your sins are forgiven," but some religious people in the crowd got angry. They said that only God could forgive sins. Jesus let them know that He had the power to forgive sins and to heal. He told the man to stand up, and he did, fully healed.

A Different Kind of Leader

A Different Kind of Leader

Jesus stopped at the booth of a tax collector named Matthew (also known as Levi) and said, "Come and follow me."

Tax collectors were not very popular with the Jewish people. Many people hated them because they worked for the Roman government and collected fees on top of the required taxes. Then they kept this extra money for themselves. Many tax collectors lived in luxury compared to the average Jewish citizen.

No doubt Matthew was surprised by Jesus' request, but he left his occupation to follow Jesus. He was so excited that he invited all of his friends to his house that night for a banquet. He wanted them to meet Jesus also.

The religious leaders could not believe their eyes when they saw Jesus at Matthew's house. Every person at the banquet was known to be a sinner. They wondered why Jesus would eat with people like that. So, Jesus told them, "I have not come to call people who think they are righteous. I have come to call those who know they are not. It isn't the healthy that need a doctor, but the sick."

One day, after spending the night praying to God, Jesus chose 12 men to be Apostles. He gave them authority to heal the sick and to cast out demons. They were:

- Peter (also called Simon Peter)
- Andrew (Peter's brother)
- James (son of Zebedee)
- John (son of Zebedee, brother of James)
- Philip
- Bartholomew
- Matthew
- Thomas
- James (son of Alphaeus)
- Judas (son of James, also called Thaddaeus)
- Simon (also called the Zealot)
- Judas Iscariot

Jesus began gathering a group of 12 men to teach, including Peter, James, and John. One of these men was named Matthew, and he was a tax collector. In those days, tax collectors often became wealthy by working for the Roman government and cheating people. So, people were surprised that Jesus would have anything to do with someone like this. Matthew had a banquet so others could come to know Jesus too, but the religious leaders wondered why Jesus would eat with sinners. Jesus stated that the healthy don't need a doctor, only the sick.

Matthew 10:1–4

Mark 2:13–17, 3:13–19

Luke 5:27–32, 6:12–16

A Special Message

One day, Jesus delivered a very special message on a hillside near the Sea of Galilee. A large number of people had come from all over Judea to hear Him speak. They wondered, "Is Jesus the Messiah? Would He reveal His plan for freeing Israel from Roman rule? Was it possible that Judea would soon be returned to its former glory? Would He tell them to take up arms and fight the Romans?"

To be fair, the Jews had reasons to hate and fear their enemies. They had suffered much under Roman rule. It had not been that long since Herod the Great had ordered the death of all the baby boys in Bethlehem. After Herod the Great's death, the kingdom had been divided between his four sons. Herod Antipas was the king of Galilee at this time, and he was not a good king either. Many people were ready to fight.

Jesus' message turned out to be quite different than expected. He began to teach them about the Kingdom of God, which has little resemblance to the kingdoms of men. Instead of fighting their enemies, Jesus wanted them to love them and to forgive them. He was telling them to be a peaceful and righteous people who served others, even if they were mistreated for doing so. "Do unto others as you would have them do to you. Be merciful because God is merciful."

Just like John the Baptist had done, Jesus taught them that it was what was in their heart that mattered to God. If they understood how much God had loved, served, and forgiven them, it should follow that they would do the same for others. Loving and obeying God is the way to be part of His Kingdom. Many religious people thought obeying the law proved that they were righteous, but their motive was to bring glory to themselves and not to God.

Jesus was inviting them to live in different way. *"You are the light of the world. A city set on a hill cannot be hidden. Nor do people light a lamp and put it under a basket, but on a stand, and it gives light to all in the house. In the same way, let your light shine before others, so that they may see your good works and give glory to your Father who is in heaven"* (Matthew 5:14).

It was a life-changing message for all who would listen.

Matthew 5–7,

Luke 6

For such a long time, the Jewish people had been oppressed by the Romans. Because of this, many thought that Jesus might be the Messiah to help them fight for freedom. Jesus wanted people to understand that His Kingdom was focused on love and forgiveness for their enemies and on being lights in this world for God.

Thread of Hope

There was nothing special about the clay vessels that held the wine of Jesus' first miracle. They were common, ordinary pots that were normally used for washing up. It was ordinary servants who were willing to do what Jesus said. They must have been filled with wonder as they drew wine out of vessels that had held only water a few minutes before. It was wine worthy of the finest celebration. Jesus had made something wonderful out of something ordinary.

It was often the poor, the rebellious, the sick, and the outcast who followed Jesus — ordinary people who had likely been neglected or rejected by the religious leaders. Just like the Samaritans, who learned that even though they had been rejected by their own relatives, they were deeply loved by God.

Jesus made it clear that He had not come for those who thought they were righteous, but for those who knew they were not. "Repent, for the kingdom of God is near," He said.

We must understand our need for a Savior before we can truly be saved.

This message offended many of the religious leaders. They had fallen into the trap of believing that people were saved by obeying the law of Moses. This led to a comparison game where some people were considered more righteous or deserving than others.

The Israelites had never been saved by keeping the law, but by their faith in a good God who accepted the blood of animals as payment for their sin (Leviticus 4:20). Because of mankind's sinful nature, the sacrifices in this God-given system had to be repeated over and over again. Though arduous, this made forgiveness possible, which in turn made whole-hearted love and gratitude to God possible as well.

The law had no power by itself. Its intent had always been to bring glory to God. Instead, people had twisted it to become a means for people to display their own goodness. We all struggle with our pride at times and must remember that we are "ordinary clay pots." Only when we are "empty" of our own claim to goodness can Jesus fill us with the "new wine" of salvation.

Then He can produce good works in us, for His glory and not ours.

Sab·bath	A day of rest, a day set aside to worship God
dis·ci·ple	a student or follower of a particular leader
a·pos·tle	twelve of Jesus' disciples who would later be sent out to carry on His ministry
syn·a·gogue	a house or place of worship in the Jewish religion

A Roman Officer's Faith

Once when Jesus was in Capernaum, a servant of one of the Roman officers in charge of the city fell ill. This was one of a very few Romans who was well-respected by the townspeople. They liked him because he had been kind to the Jews and had even built them a house of worship. The officer sent some Jews to ask Jesus to come and heal his servant. "Please come and heal this man's servant," they said, "for he has been kind to the Jews and even built our synagogue."

Jesus agreed to go, and a large crowd followed Him. While He was on the way, another servant arrived with a message from the officer. "I am not worthy to have you visit my house. That is why I have sent my servants to you instead. I know that if you give the order, my servant will be healed. For I am an officer, and when I give an order, it is followed."

Jesus was amazed. He turned to the people following Him and said, "Truly, this man has great faith. I have not seen faith like this from among my own people."

At that moment, the officer's servant was healed. This man, who some would call an enemy because of his nationality, had more faith than the people of Israel. He was a man with great authority. He could have ordered Jesus to come to his house. Instead, he humbly believed that Jesus' authority was greater than his own. His faith was so great that he knew Jesus did not even need to be physically present to perform a healing miracle.

This man clearly cared for his servants, who were likely Jewish, and when one of them was in great need, he appealed to Jesus to help him. It was not this man's position that amazed Jesus, nor was it his good deeds. As always, Jesus cared about his heart. This man's heart proved to be full of faith.

Luke 7:1–10

Though many Roman soldiers oppressed the Jewish people, there was a Roman officer who was respected by them. When one of his servants became ill, he sent some people find Jesus and ask Him to heal his servant. While Jesus was on the way, another servant came from the officer with a message. This servant said that the Roman officer did not feel worthy for Jesus to come to his house. He believed that if Jesus merely spoke the word, his servant could be healed. Jesus said He had not seen so much faith in all of Israel, and with this, He healed the officer's servant.

The Sinful Woman

One day, a religious leader named Simon asked Jesus to come to his house for a meal, and Jesus went. While He was there, a sinful woman came into the house with an expensive jar of perfume. She was crying as she knelt before Jesus. She anointed Him with the perfume and used her own hair to dry the tears that had fallen on His feet.

Simon thought to himself, "If this man were a true prophet, He would know what kind of woman this is. He would not allow a woman like this to touch Him!"

Jesus knew what Simon was thinking. "I want to tell you a story," He said. "There was a man who loaned some money to two different people. To one he loaned 500 pieces of silver, and to the other he loaned 50. Neither man could repay him. So he kindly decided to forgive the debt of both of them. Now, which do you believe loved the man more?"

"The one who owed the most," Simon said.

"You are correct," Jesus said. "When I came into your home, you did not greet me with a kiss, and you did not offer water for me to wash the dust from my feet. This woman has done what you should have done. I know she has sinned many times, but her sins have been forgiven. That is why she has shown such love for me." The woman then left in peace. Simon was left with a lot to think about.

Luke 7:36–50

As Jesus went about teaching and healing many people, He was often followed by those looked down upon by the religious leaders. One of these leaders, Simon, had Jesus over for a meal. While they were eating, a sinful woman came and anointed Jesus with an expensive perfume and wiped it up with her hair as she wept. Simon was not pleased with her, but Jesus told him a story of one who was forgiven much and one who was forgiven little. Simon knew the one forgiven much would be more grateful. Then Jesus said that this woman was forgiven much and could now go in peace.

Of Seeds and Soil

Jesus used parables to help illustrate His messages. Parables are simple stories with characters and situations the listeners could relate to. They were easy to understand on the surface, but they also had a much deeper meaning. Now, there were many who followed Jesus around simply to see what He would do next. They were curious about this unpredictable man who performed miracles. These people did not grasp or accept the true meaning of the parables. Those who were really seeking the truth would come to understand what He was saying.

One time, a large crowd of people gathered from nearby villages to hear Jesus speak, and He told them this parable:

"Once there was a farmer who scattered his seed during planting season. Some seed fell on the walkway, where it was stepped on or eaten by birds. Other seed fell on rocky ground. It sprouted and began to grow, but it soon died for lack of water. Some of the seed was choked out because it fell among the weeds. Yet, the seed that fell on fertile soil sprouted and grew into strong plants. It produced a huge crop for the farmer."

Later, Jesus explained the meaning of the four soils to His Apostles. "The seed is the word of God," He said. "The seeds that fell on the walkway represent people who hear the truth but are convinced by the devil not to believe it. The seeds that fell among the rocks represent people who hear and believe, but then they walk away as soon as they find it difficult to follow me. The seeds that fell among the weeds represent those who believe but allow the cares and pleasures of this life to be more important than my message. The seeds that fell on fertile soil represent those who hear God's word and live by it. They will produce a harvest."

It was important for the Apostles to understand this message, for one day soon they would be planting seeds of faith throughout the world.

Matthew 13:3–9, 13:18–23   *Luke 8:4–8, 8:9–15*

Mark 4:3–9, 4:13–20

Parables are simple stories that teach a lesson. One day, Jesus shared a parable about a farmer scattering seed. Some of the seed was trampled on the path, some fell on rocky soil, some were choked by weeds, but some grew strong in fertile soil. Jesus said that the seed was God's Word. People are the places, or soils, where the seed falls. Some hear the truth but don't believe. Some listen but realize the truth is too hard to follow. Some believe, but the world chokes out the truth. Some hear and believe and grow strong in God's Word.

Weeds

Jesus told a parable that had to do with planting and harvesting. He said a farmer planted good seeds of wheat, but an enemy came and scattered weeds in the field. They grew together, and the farmer felt it best to wait until the harvest to separate them. Jesus told His followers that the one who planted the seed is the Son of Man, a name He called Himself. The seeds are the people of the kingdom, and the devil is the enemy. The day will come when God's people will be separated from those who follow the devil. Until then, good and bad will have to be together.

Another parable Jesus told had to do with weeds. He said, "A farmer planted his field with good seed, but his enemy came in the middle of the night and planted weed seeds among the wheat. They sprouted and grew alongside the farmer's crop. His servants asked him if they should go through the field and pull out the weeds. Then the farmer said, 'No. You might hurt the good crop if you do that. Let them both grow together, and when the time comes, my harvesters will sort out the weeds and destroy them.' "

Later, He told His Apostles, "The one who plants the seed is the Son of Man. The good seed are the people of the Kingdom, and the field is the world. The devil is the enemy who planted the weeds, and they are his followers. The harvest is the end of the world. At that time, the Son of Man will tell his harvesters (angels) to separate the people of God's kingdom from the devil's followers. All who chose to follow the evil one will be destroyed, but the righteous will shine like the sun in their Father's Kingdom!"

Jesus often referred to Himself as the Son of Man. It was a reminder that He was a flesh-and-blood human — just like the people He had come to save. It was also a reminder of the words of the prophet Daniel:

In my vision at night I looked, and there before me was one like a son of man, coming with the clouds of heaven. He approached the Ancient of Days and was led into his presence. He was given authority, glory and sovereign power; all nations and peoples of every language worshiped him. His dominion is an everlasting dominion that will not pass away, and his kingdom is one that will never be destroyed (Daniel 7:13–14; NIV).

Matthew 13:24–30, 36–43

Wind and Waves

Jesus wanted to teach His Apostles an important lesson, so He said to them, "Let's sail to the other side of the lake." Because He was tired, Jesus fell asleep on a cushion in the back of the boat.

A powerful storm came up while they were on the lake. The waves were huge and tossed the boat around, and it began to fill with water. The men were terrified and woke Jesus up. "Wake up," they yelled, "for we are about to drown!"

Jesus stood up and said to the waves, "Quiet! Be still!" Instantly, the storm ceased. The sea became completely calm. Then He said, "Why are you afraid? Where is your faith?"

The men were astonished. They had seen Jesus perform miracles before. However, this was different. They were experienced fisherman who had no doubt been in storms before. This one must have been really fierce to make them so afraid. In their fear, they cried out to the Lord. He heard them and helped them.

"Who is this man?" they said to one another. "Even the wind and the waves obey His command!"

When they got to the other side, they met up with a man who was possessed by many demons. The local people thought he was insane and were afraid of him. So he lived alone in the cemetery outside of town. Jesus had compassion on him and cast the demons out. The man's sanity returned.

This poor man had lived alone in his misery for a very long time, but Jesus sailed a great distance to help him. At the same time, He taught His disciples that storms often come when you set out to do the will of God. Jesus would help them get through those storms if they cried out to Him, for He had power over both the natural and the spiritual worlds.

Matthew 8:23–34

Mark 4:35–41, 5:1–136

Luke 8:22–33

When journeying with His Apostles, Jesus would sometimes have them travel by boat. On one such voyage, He fell asleep in the back of the boat. A powerful storm came up, tossing the boat around, and sending waves crashing over the sides. The followers of Jesus were terrified. They cried for Him to wake up and save them. When He rose, He told the waves to be still. Immediately, the storm ceased. Then He wondered what had happened to their faith to cause them such fear. "Who is this," His followers asked, "that even the wind and waves obey Him?"

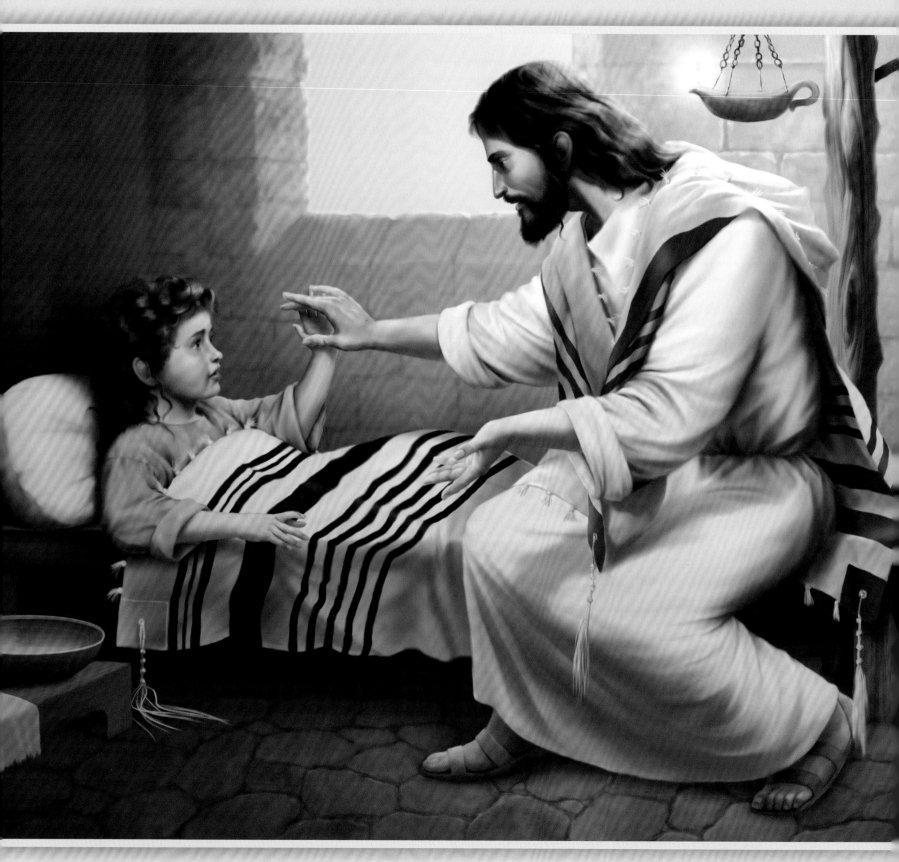

Genuine Faith

One day, a religious leader named Jairus came and fell at Jesus' feet. "My daughter is dying," he cried. "Please come and heal her so that she can live." Jesus had compassion for the man and went with him. A large group of people followed along and crowded around Jesus as He walked.

Now, there was a woman in the crowd who had been sick for 12 long years. She had spent all of her money on doctors, but no one had been able to help her. She knew that Jesus had healed many people, and she had faith to believe He could heal her also. So she pushed through the crowd and grabbed hold of the hem of Jesus' garment. She was healed in that moment. Jesus stopped walking and asked, "Who touched me?" for He had felt the healing power go out of Him. The woman fell to her knees before Jesus and told Him her story. "Your faith has healed you," He said. "Go in peace."

While this was happening, one of Jairus' servants arrived with the sad news that his daughter had died. Jesus told him, "Don't be afraid. Have faith, and she will be healed."

So Jairus took Jesus to his home, and sure enough, they found the house full of people mourning the little girl's death. Jesus asked everyone to leave except for Peter, James, John, and the girl's parents. As the little girl lay lifeless in her bed, He took her by the hand and said, "Get up, child!"

Then she did! Her life returned to her, and she stood up right before their eyes. Her parents were overcome with joy, but Jesus told them not to tell anyone what had happened. Some scholars believe He said that because His greater goal was to teach the truth about His Kingdom. He planned to travel all over the region and do just that. If word spread that He could raise the dead to life, He would not have had the time to do much traveling or teaching. Whatever His reason was, it is evident that Jesus made time for all who came to Him.

Matthew 9:18–26

Mark 5:21–43

Luke 8:40–56

A religious leader named Jairus needed Jesus because his daughter was dying. Jesus had compassion on him and started walking home with him. On their way, a woman who had been sick for 12 years reached out to touch Jesus' robe and was healed immediately. Jesus asked the people in the crowd around Him, "Who touched me?" The woman fell before Jesus, and He told her that her faith had healed her. There were mourners when Jesus arrived at Jairus' house, for his young daughter had died. So, Jesus went to her, took her by the hand, and told her to rise. She did, strong and whole again.

Sent Out

*J*esus went from village to village, teaching about the Kingdom. One day, He called his 12 Apostles together and told them it was time for them to begin their own ministry. If they split up, they could cover a lot more territory in the same amount of time, so that is what they did. He sent them out to preach to God's lost sheep, the people of Israel. They were to do as they had seen Him do. He gave them power to heal the sick, cure diseases, and cast out demons.

"Don't take any money with you," He said. "Don't even take along extra clothing or a walking stick. Trust your Heavenly Father to provide for you. Accept the hospitality of the people you meet. When you go into someone's home, give it your blessing. If they are worthy, let your blessing stand. If anyone does not welcome you, then leave that home or town behind and shake the dust of that place off of your feet. Also, beware, you could be arrested or beaten because of the message you bring. Do not be afraid if that happens. Do not worry about what to say, for the Holy Spirit of God will help you. Know this, the student is not above his teacher. Just as I will suffer for this teaching, so will you. Whoever acknowledges me before others, I will acknowledge before my Father in heaven. Whoever disowns me now, I will disown."

So the Apostles went out. They told everyone they met to repent of their sins and turn to God, and they cast out demons and healed the sick.

Matthew 10:5–42

Mark 6:6–13

Luke 9:1–6

There came a time when Jesus gathered His 12 Apostles together. He was ready to send them out to preach the good news of the Kingdom to those in Israel. The message of the Kingdom was one of power over sickness, over disease, and demons. Jesus instructed them to trust God to provide for them and to bless the homes of people who cared for their needs. They were not to worry about the message, for the Holy Spirit would guide their words. They went out in pairs, casting out demons, healing the sick, and telling all they met to repent and to come to God.

Who Do You Say that I Am?

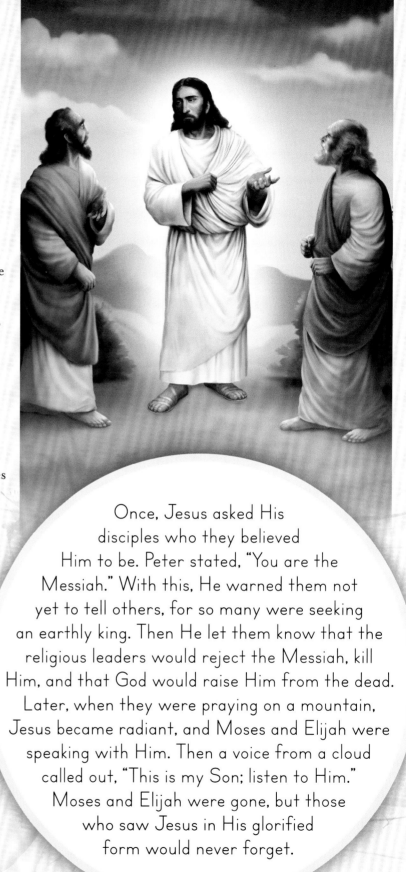

One day, Jesus asked His Apostles, "Who do you say that I am?" Peter said, "You are the Messiah!" Jesus warned them not to tell people who He was because He knew they were still looking for an earthly king, but it was important the Apostles understand, for difficult times were coming.

"The Son of Man will be rejected by the religious leaders. They will execute him, but He will be raised from the dead after three days," He told them.

A few days later, He took Peter, James, and John up on a mountain to pray. As He was praying, a great light shone all around Him. His face became radiant, and his clothing glowed with light. All of a sudden, Moses and Elijah appeared and began to speak with Jesus about the things that would soon happen.

Peter and the others were amazed and terrified. Then a cloud overshadowed them, and they heard a voice speaking from within the cloud, "This is my Son, my Chosen One; listen to him!" The Apostles fell face down on the ground in awe. Then Jesus came over and touched them and told them to get up. When they did, they found that Moses, Elijah, and the cloud had gone. They were once again alone with Jesus.

Jesus had allowed these three men to see Him in His glorified form so they would come to understand that His Kingdom was not an earthly kingdom. Many years later, both Peter and John would write about this supernatural experience. They had seen the glory and majesty of Christ.

›› *Matthew 17:1–8*

›› *Mark 9:2–8*

›› *Luke 9:20–22, 9:28–36*

›› *John 1:14*

›› *2 Peter 1:16–18*

Once, Jesus asked His disciples who they believed Him to be. Peter stated, "You are the Messiah." With this, He warned them not yet to tell others, for so many were seeking an earthly king. Then He let them know that the religious leaders would reject the Messiah, kill Him, and that God would raise Him from the dead. Later, when they were praying on a mountain, Jesus became radiant, and Moses and Elijah were speaking with Him. Then a voice from a cloud called out, "This is my Son; listen to Him." Moses and Elijah were gone, but those who saw Jesus in His glorified form would never forget.

Teach Us to Pray

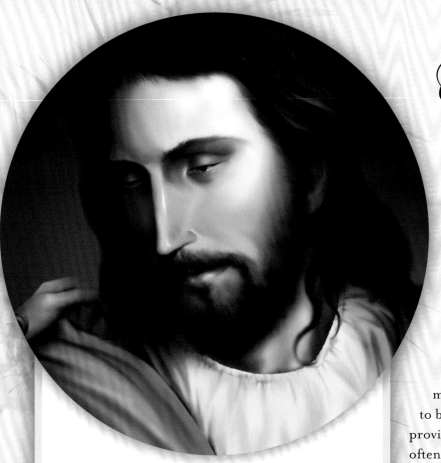

One day, Jesus' Apostles asked Him to teach them to pray.
So, He told them, *"Pray like this:*

Our Father in heaven,
may your name be kept holy.
May your Kingdom come soon.
May your will be done on earth,
as it is in heaven.
Give us today the food we need,
and forgive us our sins,
as we have forgiven those who sin against us.
And don't let us yield to temptation,
but rescue us from the evil one" (Matthew 6:9–13; NLT).

He was not telling His disciples that they always had to pray using these words. He was giving an example of what a heartfelt prayer to their Heavenly Father might look like. It might include words of praise, a desire for God's perfect will to be done, repentance for sin, and requests for protection and provision. Jesus demonstrated the importance of prayer by praying often Himself. Sometimes He went off alone to pray, and sometimes He prayed in public.

He also taught them to keep on praying. "Suppose someone came to your home for a visit and you did not have any food to serve them. So you go to a neighbor's house intending to borrow some bread, but your neighbor has already gone to bed. 'The door is locked for the night, I cannot help you,' he says. I tell you this, if you keep knocking and asking, he will eventually get up and give you the food. So don't give up asking your Heavenly Father for what you need."

For everyone who asks, receives.
Everyone who seeks, finds.
And to everyone who knocks, the door will be opened (Matthew 7:8; NLT).

> Matthew 6:9–15
> Luke 11:1–13
> Revelation 3:20

The Apostles wanted to know how to pray, so they asked Jesus to teach them. He told them they should pray by focusing first on God and His holiness, desiring His kingdom to come, and praying for His will to be done on earth. They were then to ask God for what they needed each day and to be forgiving as much as they wanted to be forgiven by Him. Finally, they were to ask God to help them overcome temptation and to defeat the evil one. Jesus added that they should pray continually, seeking God's help and guidance, as one desperately seeks help from a friend or neighbor.

Thread of Hope

It might be easy to think that all of the religious leaders were against Jesus. Yet, we have read about Nicodemus, Simon, and Jairus, all of whom were at least willing to listen and engage with Him. This could not have been easy for them. After all, they were highly educated and well versed in the Jewish religion. It was all they had ever known.

Still yet, these men watched Jesus work, and they listened to His words. He spoke with such authority. His words brought about real change, in both the natural and the spiritual realms. He had even brought Jairus' daughter back to life. We can only imagine the conversations they must have had. Who is this man? How is He able to perform these signs and wonders? Could He really be the Messiah? But He is threatening our authority and our way of life? What shall we do?

Jesus cared about both the physical and spiritual needs of everyone He met, even the religious leaders. He taught Simon a powerful lesson on forgiveness and judging. Simon had invited Jesus to his home, when a sinful woman burst into the house. She wept and knelt before Jesus. Yet, Simon felt the need to point out the woman's sins.

Simon had already passed judgment on her, but Jesus offered her forgiveness, and with that came hope for a new life. "Your faith has saved you; go in peace," He told her (Luke 7:50). God loves because it is His nature to love — so much so that He was willing to forgive this woman of her many sins. She knew she did not deserve His mercy, and her heart filled with love and gratitude to the point of washing His feet with her tears.

It is never a good idea to compare ourselves to other people. If we compare ourselves to a perfect God, we will have the humility to understand that we all fall short. We all need forgiveness. Simon needed to see his own self-righteousness. We are left to wonder what he did with this important lesson.

Jesus also shared a life-changing message with Nicodemus when He told him he must be born again. Jesus was talking about a spiritual birth. That birth happens when someone repents of their sin and places their faith in Jesus as Lord and Savior. What follows is peace and joy at knowing they are forgiven and will spend eternity in heaven. It should also make them more forgiving of others.

After salvation, a person might look the same on the outside, but their heart and mind will be different. This is what it means to become a new creation in Christ, or to be born again.

par·a·ble | a short story with a moral theme or lesson

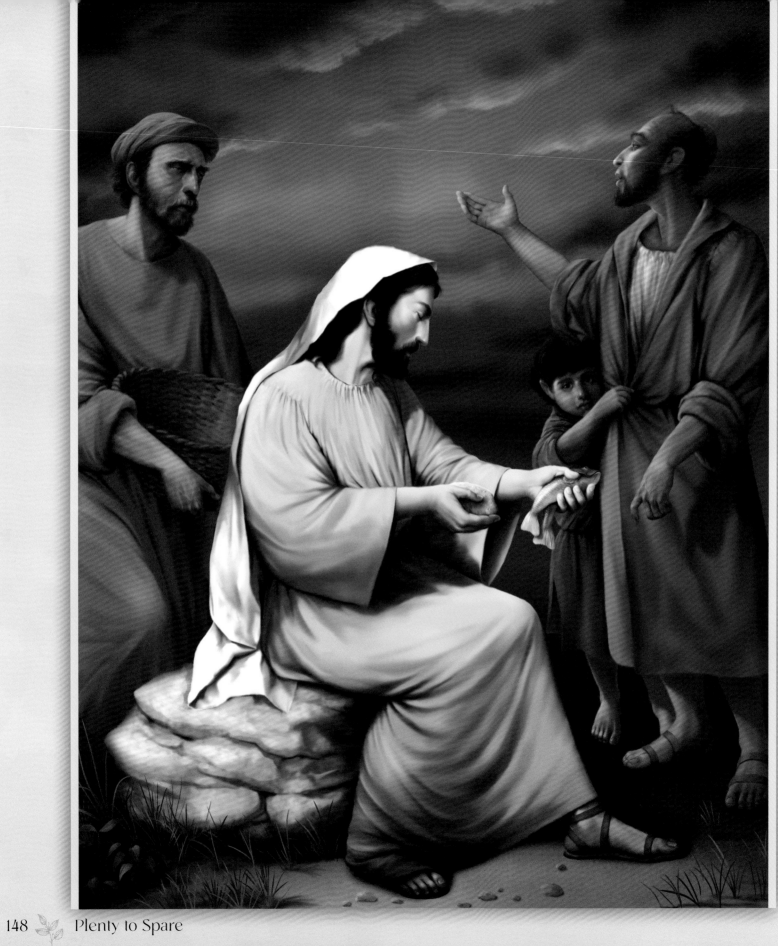

Plenty to Spare

Plenty to Spare

Jesus learned that John the Baptist, while he was in prison, had been executed. Wanting a little time alone, Jesus went off by Himself, but the crowds soon found Him. Naturally, Jesus did not turn them away. Later on, His Apostles asked Him to send the crowd away to find something to eat and a place to stay. Jesus replied, "You feed them."

"With what?" they asked. Then Andrew said, "There is a young boy with five loaves of bread and two fish. What good is that with this many people?"

There were about 5,000 men, not including women and children. Jesus told them to sit in groups of 50 or so people. When everyone was seated, Jesus took the bread and the fish and looked up to heaven. He blessed the food and then handed it to His Apostles to distribute. The food never ran out. Everyone ate until they were full. They even picked up 12 baskets of leftovers!

The people were in awe of Jesus. They had seen Him heal people. They had seen Him cast out demons. However, this was something entirely different. He miraculously supplied food for thousands of people in a moment's time! Their king had never done any of these things. They were ready to replace Herod Antipas and crown Jesus King of Judea, by force if necessary.

Then Jesus slipped away from them, for they did not yet understand the true purpose of His Kingdom or His coming. He was not that kind of king.

- Matthew 14:13–21
- Mark 6:30–44
- Luke 9:10–17
- John 6:1–15

Jesus found out that John the Baptist had been executed, so He went off to find a quiet place to be alone. The crowds followed Jesus, and because of His compassion, He let them stay. Later, the Apostles came and said that the crowds should leave to find food. Jesus told them to feed the people. All they could find was a boy with five fish and two loaves of bread. There were over 5,000 people to feed! Jesus blessed the food, and the Apostles gave it to the people. Not only was there enough for everyone, there were 12 baskets of leftovers!

"I Am the Bread of Life"

The next day, the crowd found Him on the other side of the lake. "Why did you come over here?" they asked Him.

"You want to be with me because I gave you bread, not because you understand my message and miracles. Don't worry about what you will eat. Instead, spend your time and energy seeking eternal life. Believe what I am telling you. Just as my Heavenly Father gave the Israelites manna to eat in the desert, he offers you the true bread from heaven."

"We want that bread every day," they replied. Of course, they were thinking about food, like the bread and fish He had given them the day before. So, Jesus explained further.

I am the bread of life. Whoever comes to me will never go hungry, and whoever believes in me will never be thirsty. But as I told you, you have seen me and still you do not believe. All those the Father gives me will come to me, and whoever comes to me I will never drive away. For I have come down from heaven not to do my will but to do the will of him who sent me. And this is the will of him who sent me, that I shall lose none of all those he has given me, but raise them up at the last day. For my Father's will is that everyone who looks to the Son and believes in him shall have eternal life, and I will raise them up at the last day
(John 6:35–40; NIV).

The next day after Jesus had fed so many by His miracle, the crowds found Him again. They began asking for more food from Him. Then He began to speak with them about bread, but not simply the bread you eat for your body's strength. This was about Him being the Bread of Life that had come from heaven. This Bread of Life can feed a person's soul and gives eternal life to all who believe in Jesus. Even though Jesus had shown His compassion and His power, many left Him at this time because He was teaching about heavenly things they simply did not understand.

This was a difficult message, and they began to question Jesus' words. How could this man claim that He had come down from heaven? Wasn't this the son of Joseph and Mary?

Jesus told them, "No one can come to me unless the Father draws them. I am telling the truth. Anyone who believes in me will have eternal life." He wanted them to understand who He was and why He had come. Believing in Him was like eating spiritual food — it would strengthen and encourage them in this life, but it would also give them eternal life. Not everyone believed Him, and many people deserted Him at this time.

John 6:22–34

The Blind Man Sees

One day when He was teaching in the temple courts, Jesus said, *I am the light of the world. Whoever follows me will not walk in darkness, but will have the light of life* (John 8:12).

Not long after this, Jesus and His followers came upon a man who had been born blind. "Why was this man born blind?" His followers asked. "Was it because of his own sin or that of his parents?"

Jesus replied, "Neither. This happened so that you might witness the power of God." Then He spat on the ground and spread the wet earth over the man's eyes. "Go wash this off in the pool of Siloam," He told him. As soon as the man did, he was healed from his blindness!

This happened on the Sabbath, so it upset the religious leaders. Some of them said, "This man could not be from God because he is working on the Sabbath!" Others said, "An ordinary man could not perform such a miracle!" So they were divided in their opinions about Jesus and argued with one another.

The blind man said, "Since the world began, no one has been able to restore the sight of someone born blind. This man could not have healed me unless he came from God."

Then Jesus asked the man who had been healed, "Do you believe I am the Son of Man?"

"Yes, I believe!" the man said, and he worshiped Jesus.

This man gained his physical sight and his spiritual sight in the same day. "I came for this reason," Jesus said, "to give sight to the blind, and to show those who think they see clearly that they do not, for they are spiritually blind."

John 9

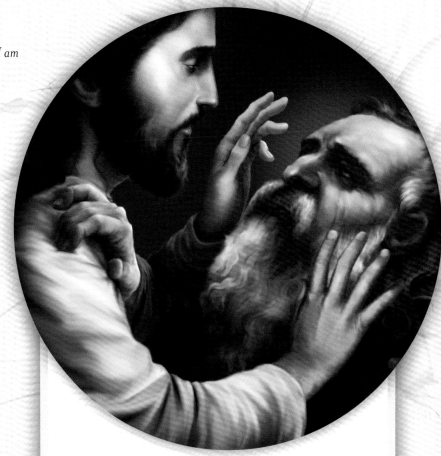

One day, Jesus was teaching in the temple courts about how He was the light of the world. He and His followers walked past a man who was born blind. The followers of Jesus wondered if the man was blind because of his own sin or his parents' sin. Jesus said it was not because of sin but so that they might see the power of God. So, Jesus took some mud and pressed it to the man's eyes and told him to wash in the pool of Siloam. When he did, he could see again. The religious leaders looked down on Jesus, but the man worshiped Him.

A Better View

A Better View

Whenever Jesus was in a certain town, people would line the streets in order to see Him. One time, there was a man named Zacchaeus, who was too short to see over the crowd. He was a very clever man, so he climbed a big tree to get a better view. Then he waited for Jesus to come.

Zacchaeus was the chief tax collector in that region, and he was very rich. When Jesus walked by, He looked up into the tree and said, "Zacchaeus, come down, for I must be a guest in your home today." Zacchaeus was so excited! He climbed down immediately and took Jesus to his home.

The other townspeople were not happy about this. They did not like Zacchaeus because he had made himself rich with their money. "Why would Jesus go to the home of such a bad man?" they wondered. Zacchaeus was so moved by the Lord's acceptance of him that he said, "I will give back four times as much money to all the people I have cheated, and I will give half my wealth to the poor." Zacchaeus was a changed man.

"Salvation has come to this house today," Jesus said. "Zacchaeus has shown himself to be a true son of Abraham. I came to seek people just like him."

Jesus made it clear to everyone that His love and acceptance are not reserved for any particular group of people.

Luke 19:1–10

Crowds of people always followed Jesus, which meant it was sometimes hard to get near Him. A tax collector named Zacchaeus, a short man, had an even harder time seeing Jesus. So he climbed a tree to see Him better. Jesus looked up in the tree and told Zacchaeus that He wanted to go to his house right then. Zacchaeus climbed down, excited to have time with Jesus, but the crowds hated this because he was a tax collector. Zacchaeus knew he had cheated people and promised to return their money and give money to the poor as well. Jesus was pleased.

The Lost Ones

Though Jesus often spoke to the crowds, at times He spoke directly to the religious leaders. Jesus told them several parables that shared God's heart for the lost people in the world. One story was about a man with a hundred sheep who lost one. Another was about a woman who had ten coins but lost one. A final story was about a man who had two sons. One of his sons left his father and was lost in the world. Each story showed the value of what was lost and the joy that came when it was found. This is the heart of God.

The religious leaders did not like that Jesus spent time with tax collectors and sinners. He had even been seen eating with them. They believed it was wrong to do that. So, Jesus told them a series of stories.

"Suppose a man has a hundred sheep but one of them runs away. Would he not leave the 99 behind in the sheepfold and go searching for the lost one? And when he finds it, won't he lovingly carry it back home? Or imagine that a woman has ten silver coins and loses one. Would she not search high and low through her house until she finds it? Would she not be joyful when she does? You should know that there is more joy in heaven over a sinner who repents and turns to God than there is for the 99 who have not run away. Even the angels rejoice when this happens!"

Finally, to make sure they understood His message, He told them a parable about a lost son. In this story, a man had two sons. The younger son took his inheritance and left home. He blew all his money on sinful living and eventually ended up with nothing. When he could no longer find food to eat, he headed for his father's house, intending to beg for his mercy. When his father saw him coming, he ran to greet his son and welcomed him home with great joy.

Now, the older brother had never left his father. Therefore, he believed he was more deserving of his father's love and blessings. He was angry when his father forgave his brother and welcomed him back into the family.

The religious leaders realized that they were the "older brother" Jesus was referring to in this story. They did not appreciate the comparison.

Luke 15:1–31

Religious Leaders Want to Stone Jesus

One day, Jesus was at the temple in Jerusalem. It was during the Festival of Dedication, and many Jews had gathered there. They kept asking Him if He was the Messiah. "How long will you keep us in suspense? Are you the Messiah or not?" they said.

"I have already answered that question, but you didn't believe me. The work I do in my Father's name proves that what I say is true. You don't believe because you are not my sheep. My sheep hear my voice and listen. I know them, and they know and follow me. My Father has given them to me, and no one can take them away, for the Father and I are one."

The religious leaders were growing desperate. They were tired of Jesus stirring up the people.

So after He said this, they picked up stones to kill Him. Then Jesus said, "For which of my good works are you going to kill me? I have done only what my Father directed me to do."

"It is not because of your good works," they said, "but because you claim to be God. That is a great sin!"

Jesus replied, "The Father sent me into the world to do His work. If you don't believe my words, then believe because of the miracles I have performed. I could not have done them unless the Father and I are one."

These religious leaders still did not believe. Instead, they tried to seize Jesus, but He escaped through the crowd. He crossed over the Jordan River and stayed there for a time, and many people there believed in Him.

The leaders considered Jesus an enemy of the Jewish people and their religion, and they were determined to stop Him.

John 10:22–42

Many of the religious leaders had grown impatient with Jesus. They felt that He stirred up the people against them, even though He was only showing them the true heart of God. When He spoke of God as His Father, and that He and the Father were one, it was more than these leaders could take. Picking up stones, they came to kill Him for claiming He was God. Because it was not yet His time to die, Jesus slipped away through the crowd. He crossed the Jordon River and stayed there for a time. The Jewish leaders began plotting how they could stop Jesus for good.

  Lazarus, Come Out!

Lazarus, Come Out!

Not long after, Jesus learned that one of His friends had become ill. Lazarus and his sisters, Martha and Mary, lived in Bethany. When Lazarus got sick, Martha and Mary sent word to Jesus, "Lord, please come quickly. Lazarus is very sick."

When He got the message, Jesus told His Apostles that Lazarus' illness had happened so that the Son of God would be glorified. Even though He cared very much for Lazarus and his sisters, Jesus stayed where He was for two more days. Then He told His Apostles it was time to head back to Jerusalem, but they would stop in Bethany on the way.

"Wait," they said, "you almost got stoned there — why would you want to go back?"

Jesus responded, "Lazarus has died, and for your sakes, I am glad we were not there. Now you will really believe."

When they arrived, they learned that Lazarus had already been in his grave for four days. Many people from Jerusalem had come to mourn with Martha and Mary. When Martha heard that Jesus had come, she ran to meet Him. "Lord, if only you had been here. Then my brother would not have died," she said. Jesus replied,

I am the resurrection and the life.
Whoever believes in me, though he die,
yet shall he live, and everyone who lives
and believes in me shall never die.
Do you believe this? (John 11:25–26).

"Yes, I believe you are the Messiah, the one who has come into the world from God," she said. Then Martha went to get her sister, and all the mourners followed them back to where Jesus was.

When Mary saw the Lord, she fell at His feet and cried, and all the crowd was crying with her. Jesus was deeply moved by their tears, and He wept. "Take me to him," He said. When they got to the tomb, Jesus said, "Roll the stone away."

"He has been dead for four days!" Martha protested.

"Didn't I say you would see God's glory if you believe?" So they rolled the stone away, and Jesus looked up to heaven and prayed. Then He shouted, "Lazarus, come out!" To everyone's amazement, Lazarus walked out of that tomb alive and well.

John 11:1–44

A man named Lazarus, along with his sisters, Martha and Mary, were dear friends of Jesus. Lazarus became ill, and his sisters asked Jesus to come right away. Instead of leaving immediately, Jesus chose to stay where He was. As they finally left to see His friends, Jesus told His Apostles that Lazarus was dead. He had actually been in his grave for four days, and his sisters were heartbroken. Jesus told them that He was the resurrection and the life. Then He asked them to roll away the stone from the grave. Everyone stood amazed when Jesus called Lazarus, who walked out alive.

The Plot against Jesus

*L*azarus had been dead for four days, and now he was up walking around. Many of the people who had seen this miracle believed in Jesus. Others went to the religious leaders and told them what Jesus had done. So, the leading priests called the high council together. They needed to act before things got out of control.

"What can we do about this man? He has surely performed many miracles. Before long, everyone will believe in Him. If that happens, the Roman army will come and destroy our temple and our nation."

Then the high priest said, "It is better that one man die than for the entire nation to be destroyed."

From that time on, they began to plot the death of Jesus. However, Jesus and His Apostles left Jerusalem. They went to a town near the wilderness and stayed there for a while.

Now, it was almost time for the Passover, and people were coming to Jerusalem from around the country to observe the holiday. Many of them had already encountered Jesus when He had traveled to their towns. Those who had not were looking forward to seeing Him for the first time because His reputation as a teacher and healer had spread throughout the country.

The religious leaders ordered that anyone who saw Jesus was to report it immediately. They had finally come up with a plan, and if all went well, this man would not be troubling them much longer.

John 11:45–57

After Jesus raised Lazarus from the dead, many people who had seen this powerful miracle put their faith in Him. There were others who began plotting a way to stop Him. They were concerned about His influence on the Jewish people. The high priest even said it would be better if one man died in order to save the nation from being destroyed. Now, the time of Passover was nearing, and crowds would soon be filling the city of Jerusalem. Many were hoping to see Jesus in order to know Him more. Others were watching for Him so they could put an end to His life.

Light in the Darkness

Jesus knew that His life was in danger, but He chose to return to Jerusalem for Passover anyway. He told His Apostles, "A kernel of wheat must die before it can produce a harvest. It dies when it is planted in the ground, but its death brings about new life."

News that He was nearing the city swept through the area, and a large crowd of people flocked to meet Him. They lined the road with their cloaks as He rode into town on the back of a donkey's colt. The people waved palm branches and shouted, "Praise God! Blessings on the one who comes in the name of the Lord! Hail to Israel's King!"

The city was in an uproar, but not everyone in the crowd supported Jesus. Despite all the miracles He had performed, there were still a lot of people who refused to believe He was the Messiah. Now, there were also people who did believe, but they were afraid to admit it for fear of what others would think of them. Then there were those who wanted Him dead.

Despite this, Jesus did not sneak into town. Instead, He rode into town publicly and shouted for all to hear,

If you trust me, you are trusting not only me, but also God who sent me. For when you see me, you are seeing the one who sent me. I have come as a light to shine in this dark world, so that all who put their trust in me will no longer remain in the dark.

I will not judge those who hear me but don't obey me, for I have come to save the world and not to judge it. But all who reject me and my message will be judged on the day of judgment by the truth I have spoken. I don't speak on my own authority. The Father who sent me has commanded me what to say and how to say it. And I know his commands lead to eternal life; so I say whatever the Father tells me to say (John 12:44–50; NLT).

- Matthew 21:1–12
- John 12:12–18, 24, 37–50
- Zechariah 9:9

Jesus and His Apostles intended to go to Jerusalem for the Passover, even though He knew that many religious leaders had planned to trap Him. He told His followers that a kernel of wheat must be planted in the ground and die before it can grow into something that gives life. He spoke this about His own life. The crowds knew Jesus was coming, and they lined the roads, shouting praises to God and calling Jesus their King. He rode into the city on a donkey's colt, and the people covered the road with their cloaks in such joy. Here was Jesus, a light shining in the darkness.

Thread of Hope

Israel had failed in its mission to be a light to the world. They were not even a light to themselves. Throughout their history, none of their leaders had managed to bring about a devotion to God that had stood the test of time.

Jesus claimed to be "the light of the world." He had come to accomplish what people could not. He lived a life of perfect obedience to God. At the same time, He also gave proof of His own divine authority.

While only a fraction of His life has been covered in *God's Story,* the New Testament is full of the miraculous works and words of Jesus. He gave sight to the blind, He opened the ears of the deaf and the mouths of the mute, He restored those who were sick or lame, and He gave new life to the dead. He cast out demons, fed the hungry, and loved the outcasts.

All of these things happened to real people. There are spiritual lessons in their stories that should not be missed. All people have been "born blind" spiritually and have been handicapped by sin. To all who repent and believe, Jesus will give the ability to see, hear, and understand spiritual truth. He will open their eyes and ears. Then He will empower them to trust and obey Him. He restores what is lame and gives new life.

It is not surprising that people resist this message, for it goes against our sinful nature, where people can decide for themselves what is right and what is wrong. Even many of Israel's religious leaders interpreted the Law of Moses to suit themselves and judge others. They believed they had earned the right to enter God's Kingdom by their good works. Jesus challenged them like no one had before, and they did not like it. Human pride had gotten the best of them.

It was the people who understood and accepted their brokenness who were healed and restored, just like Zacchaeus, who was changed by his encounter with the Lord, everyone deserves the chance to meet Jesus. We never know how they might respond.

God loves everyone, including those who hate Him. So, in His final entrance into Jerusalem, Jesus appealed to everyone present, *"I have come as a light to shine in this dark world, so that all who put their trust in me will no longer remain in the dark"* (John 12:46; NLT).

su·per·nat·u·ral	a spiritual force
glo·ri·fy	to give honor, praise, or worship to

Obstacles and Offerings

After He arrived in Jerusalem, Jesus made His way to the temple. Once again, He found that a marketplace had been constructed on the temple grounds. Booths and merchants were in the way of those who had truly come to worship God. They were obstacles. So Jesus sent them out of the temple. "God's temple is a place for prayer, but you have turned it into a den of thieves!" He said.

When evening came, Jesus left the city, but He returned to the temple the next day. As He was on the way, the religious leaders asked Him many questions. They tried to trick Him into saying something that was against the law so that they could have Him arrested.

A teacher of the law heard them debating and asked Jesus which was the most important commandment. Jesus responded,

'Hear O Israel: The Lord our God, the Lord is one. And you shall love the Lord your God with all your heart and with all your soul and with all your mind and with all your strength.' The second is this: 'You shall love your neighbor as yourself.' There is no other commandment greater than these (Mark 12:29–31).

No one could argue with His answer. From then on, the religious leaders stopped asking Jesus questions, but they still wanted Him dead. Then Jesus turned to the crowd and said, "These leaders like the respect they receive because of their position. They enjoy their seats at the head of the table, yet they cheat widows out of their money. Then they go and make long prayers in public. Beware of these men."

Soon after He said this, Jesus noticed some wealthy people placing large offerings in the collection box. Then a poor widow came along and dropped in two small coins.

Jesus said, "I tell you the truth, this woman has given more than all the others. For she has given everything she has, but the others have only given a tiny part of their surplus."

As if on cue, this poor widow had come along and provided the perfect example of Jesus' message. It was not the super religious, nor the wealthy, who were following the great commandment. It was a poor woman with a big heart and a lot of faith. Her offering may have been small from the world's perspective, but it touched the heart of God.

> Matthew 21:12–17

> Mark 11:15–19, 12:35–44

> Luke 19:45–48, 21:1–4

> Jeremiah 7:9–11

After Jesus entered Jerusalem, He came to the temple only to find merchants filling the space meant for prayer. Jesus drove them out, which caused the religious leaders to hate Him even more. He made sure people knew that many of these leaders did not please God, for what they did was done to impress others. Jesus even observed this at the place where people gave offerings to God. The wealthy made large contributions for everyone to see, but a poor woman came and gave just two small coins. Jesus said she gave more than the others because she gave from all she had.

Jesus Teaches About the Future

Jesus Teaches about the Future

As Jesus was leaving the temple that day, He told His Apostles, "These buildings will one day be destroyed. Not a single stone will be left standing on top of another."

The temple grounds were magnificent. It was an impressive site with beautiful buildings and architecture. Later that day, the Apostles asked Jesus when the destruction of the temple would happen. "You must be careful," He told them. "Many people will come in my name to try and deceive you. There will be wars all over the world, and earthquakes and famine. These things must happen, but the end won't follow right away. For the good news must be preached to all nations before I return. It will be a difficult time, but those who remain faithful to me will be saved. It will be like it was in Noah's time. People went about as they normally did until Noah entered the ark. Then the flood came and destroyed them.

"Don't be fooled by people who claim to be the Messiah. Or who say, 'Look, he is over here or over there.' For when the Son of Man returns, the sun will become dark and the moon will not give its light. The stars will fall from the sky, and the powers of heaven will be shaken. Then everyone will see the Son of Man coming on the clouds with power and glory. Only the Father knows the exact hour of my return. So always stay alert and be ready!"

It is not hard to imagine that the Apostles believed all of these things would happen in their lifetime. Jesus had warned them that His death was drawing near, but they still did not understand that His death would take away the need for a physical temple. For one day soon, the Holy Spirit would come to dwell within those who placed their faith in Jesus. His people would become His temple.

There would be difficult days ahead for the followers of Jesus, but He gave them hope by telling them that He would return one day. He did not tell them the hour of His return. Instead, He told them to stay alert and remain faithful.

It was a message for all believers for all time.

> Matthew 24:1–51

> Mark 13:1–37

> Luke 21:1–4

Walking with His Apostles from the beautiful temple area, Jesus mentioned to them that every stone of the buildings would one day be torn down. The Apostles were concerned and wondered when this might happen. Jesus told them that there would be many signs of the last days, such as wars, earthquakes, and famine. Through it all, Jesus told them that the good news of salvation would be preached to all nations, and after that, He would return.

The Last Supper

The Last Supper

It was soon time to eat the Passover meal, and Jesus and His Apostles were sharing this special time together. As they reclined at the table, Jesus said, "I have been waiting to share this moment with you. For I will not eat this meal again until its true purpose is fulfilled in the Kingdom of God."

He took some bread and wine and, giving thanks to God, said, "Eat and drink, for this represents my body that will be broken for you and my blood that will be shed for you. For the Son of Man must die, and the one who will betray him is sitting at this very table."

Then He gave a piece of bread to Judas Iscariot and told him, "Go, and do what you have planned to do."

Then He said to the rest of them, "I will not be with you much longer. The time has come for the Son of Man to enter into His glory. I am giving you a new commandment. Love each other as I have loved you. Your love for each other will prove to the world that you are my disciples.

"Now don't be afraid. Trust God and trust me. I am going to my Father's house, but there is more than enough room there for you too. I will prepare a place for you, and when the time is right I will come get you."

…I am the way, the truth, and the life.
No one can come to the Father except through me (John 14:6; NLT).

Jesus spent the evening talking with the Apostles. He reminded them that His Kingdom was not like the world's kingdom. In the world, kings and great men had many servants. In God's Kingdom, it is better to serve than to be served. That is the mark of a true follower of Christ. He also warned them that some people would hate them for following Him.

"The world loves those that belong to it, but that no longer describes you. For I have called you out of the world so that you can show others the way to Me and My Kingdom," He said. "Some will listen to you, but many will not. They will even mistreat you because of your loyalty to me. I have proven myself to them by performing miracles in their sight. I did things that no one else could do, but they have still chosen to reject and hate me without cause. Know that after I am gone, I will send the Holy Spirit to you. He will never leave you. He will lead you to the truth and help you to remain strong."

Matthew 20:25–27

Matthew 26:17–30

Mark 14:12–26

Luke 22:15–27

John 14–16

The time came for the Passover meal, and Jesus spent this time with His Apostles. He began teaching them through symbols what would be happening to Him soon. He took some bread, gave it to them to eat, and told them that it represented His body that would be broken. He took some wine, gave it to them to drink, and told them that it represented His blood that would be shed. He told Judas to go and do what he planned to do — betray Jesus. Then He taught the remaining Apostles about His sacrifice and about sending the Holy Spirit so they would never be alone.

Prayers in a Garden

Later that evening, Jesus warned Peter that Satan would try and tempt him to abandon his faith. "I have prayed that your faith will not fail," He said. "Once you have repented and returned to Me, help your brothers to remain strong."

"I am ready to go to prison with you if that is necessary. Or even to die with you!" Peter said.

Then Jesus told him, "Peter, before the rooster crows tomorrow, you will deny three times that you even know Me."

Meanwhile, Judas had gone to the religious leaders and offered to help them carry out their plan to arrest Jesus. In exchange, they gave him 30 pieces of silver.

Now, Jesus had gone to the Garden of Gethsemane with Peter, James, and John to pray. He told His friends, "My soul is very troubled. Keep watch with me while I pray." Then He fell to the ground and cried out to God. "Father, must I go through this suffering? Yet, I want your will to be done and not mine."

Jesus noticed that His friends had fallen asleep. "Stay alert and pray so that you are not overcome with temptation," He told them. Twice more He went off to pray alone and His friends fell asleep. Then He woke them up and said, "Get up, for the time has come. Here comes my betrayer!"

Just then, Judas arrived with a mob of people armed with clubs and swords. Included in this mob were Jewish priests and temple guards. Judas had told them to arrest the man that he greeted with a kiss. He walked up to Jesus and said, "Greetings, Teacher!" Then he kissed Him on the cheek.

So Jesus was arrested and taken to the home of the high priest, where many of the religious leaders had gathered.

› Matthew 26:14–16, 26:36–56

› Mark 14:26, 32–52

› Luke 22:33–53

Judas had left the others during the Passover meal and gone to the religious leaders. They paid him to tell them where Jesus was going to be so they could arrest Him. Jesus and some of the other Apostles soon made their way to a garden called Gethsemane so they could pray. Jesus was troubled by what He knew was about to happen. As He sought help from God, His followers kept falling asleep. Then Judas came with a mob of people, including the religious leaders, and they arrested Jesus. Then the followers of Jesus ran away as He was led to the high priest.

Denial and Trial

The religious leaders questioned Jesus throughout the night, trying to get Him to say something worthy of the death penalty. While this was happening, Peter made his way into the courtyard and warmed himself by the fire. He wanted to know what was happening to the Lord. A servant girl recognized him and said, "You are a follower of Jesus." Peter denied it. Then she began telling the others in the courtyard, "This man is a follower of Jesus!" Again, Peter denied it. A little later some of the others in the crowd accused him, but Peter said, "I do not even know this man!" At that moment, he heard a rooster crowing. Peter began to cry, and he left the courtyard, remembering the words Jesus had spoken to him earlier that evening.

When the leaders had finished questioning Jesus, they took Him to the Roman governor, Pontius Pilate, to face charges. When he learned that Jesus was from Galilee, he sent Him to stand trial before Herod Antipas instead, who was the king of Galilee. Jesus refused to defend Himself. So Herod Antipas and his soldiers mocked and ridiculed Jesus then sent Him back to Pilate.

Now, Pilate believed that the religious leaders were jealous of Jesus. He wanted to let Him go, but the leaders pressured him to order the execution anyway. They stirred the local people into an uproar so that they cried out, "Crucify Him! Crucify Him!"

Pilate did not want a riot to start because that would make him look like a poor leader, and he feared losing his position as governor. He tried one more time to convince the people that Jesus was not a criminal. He offered them a way out of their misguided anger. It was a tradition to show mercy to one Jewish prisoner every year during Passover. So, Pilate offered to release Jesus. The crowd responded by yelling, "Don't release Him! Crucify Him! Crucify Him!"

So he sent for a bowl of water and made a show of washing his hands in front of the crowd. "The burden for this man's death lies with you," he said. "I take no responsibility." Then he had Jesus whipped and turned Him over to Roman soldiers to be crucified. The soldiers mocked Him. They stuck a crown made of thorns on His head and dressed Him in a purple robe and shouted, "Hail! The King of the Jews!"

➢ *Matthew 26, 27*   ➢ *Luke 22, 23*

➢ *Mark 14, 15*   ➢ *John 18*

The trial of Jesus took place at night, in secret. The religious leaders wanted Him to confess to anything that might help them have Him put to death. When they were done questioning Him, they led Him to Pilate, the Roman governor, for they needed his approval. He sent Jesus to Herod Antipas, the king of Galilee, but Herod returned Jesus to Pilate for sentencing. Pilate did not believe Jesus had done anything worthy of death, but the crowds were shouting, "Crucify him!" Not wishing to upset the Jewish leaders, Pilate ordered Jesus to be whipped, then turned Him over to the Roman soldiers to execute Him.

A Deep Darkness

The soldiers spat on Jesus and they beat Him with a whip before parading Him through the streets of Jerusalem. They forced Him to pick up His own cross and haul it on His beaten and bloody back to a place outside the city called Golgotha. Then, as the people watched, they nailed His hands and feet to the cross He had carried. Finally, they placed a sign above His head that said, THIS IS JESUS, THE KING OF THE JEWS, and raised the cross up high. Two other men were crucified at the same time, one on His right and the other on His left.

As He hung there, Jesus could see the faces of those who had wanted Him dead. He watched as soldiers divided His clothing among themselves. He said, "Forgive them, Father, for they don't know what they are doing."

This all happened at nine o'clock in the morning. Many people passed by and insulted Jesus, including the religious leaders. "He saved others, but He cannot save Himself," they said.

At noontime, a deep darkness fell across the land. It was as if nature itself was in mourning and the sun refused to shine. Suddenly, at three o'clock in the afternoon, as if in protest, an earthquake caused the ground to shake violently. The great curtain that separated the Holy of Holies from the rest of the temple was torn in two. This could not have been done by human hands, for the curtain was woven of thick cloth and reached to the very top of the temple, which was several stories tall.

It had been torn from top to bottom.

At that moment, Jesus cried out to God, "Father, I entrust my spirit to you." Then He died.

The Roman officer who had supervised the crucifixion was amazed by these events. "Surely, this man was the Son of God!" he said. Other people witnessed these events as well, including those who had called for Jesus' death.

Matthew 27:33–37

Mark 15:22–26

Luke 23:33–34

John 19:17–30

Psalm 22

Isaiah 53:4–6

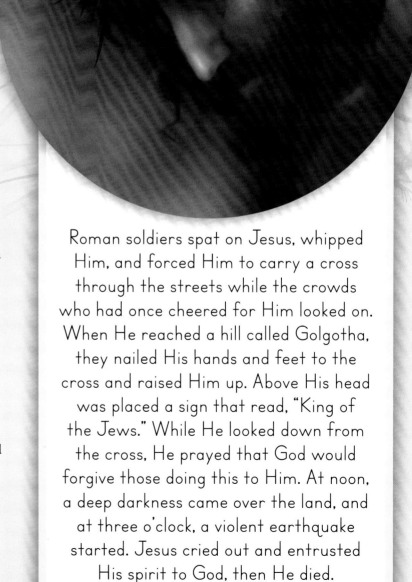

Roman soldiers spat on Jesus, whipped Him, and forced Him to carry a cross through the streets while the crowds who had once cheered for Him looked on. When He reached a hill called Golgotha, they nailed His hands and feet to the cross and raised Him up. Above His head was placed a sign that read, "King of the Jews." While He looked down from the cross, He prayed that God would forgive those doing this to Him. At noon, a deep darkness came over the land, and at three o'clock, a violent earthquake started. Jesus cried out and entrusted His spirit to God, then He died.

After Jesus died, a man named Joseph of Arimathea asked the governor if he could bury Jesus' body. He was given permission, and with the help of Nicodemus, they laid Jesus' body in Joseph's tomb, rolling a stone across the entrance. Because some religious leaders were concerned that Jesus' followers might steal His body, they had armed guards placed at the entrance. On Sunday morning, several women came to the tomb. What they saw startled them. The guards had passed out from fear, and there by the tomb was an angel, bright as lightning. The angel told the women not to be afraid, for Jesus had risen.

Don't Be Afraid

Now, there was a good man named Joseph of Arimathea who had become a disciple of Jesus. He was also a member of the Jewish High Council, but he had not agreed with the actions of the other religious leaders. When he saw that Jesus had died, he went to the governor and asked for His body. Then he and Nicodemus (the same man who had previously visited Jesus at night) buried Him in Joseph's tomb and rolled a large stone in front of the entrance.

Then the other religious leaders asked the governor to place an armed guard in front of the tomb. They were afraid that followers of Jesus would come and steal His body and then claim that He had risen from the dead. If that happened, they could end up in a worse position than before. So soldiers were sent to permanently seal the tomb and protect the burial site.

The next day was pretty quiet because it was the Sabbath. Jesus' followers gathered together in a secret location because they were afraid of the religious leaders. After the Sabbath passed, Mary Magdalene and some other women went to visit the tomb. They were very sad, but as they drew near, they saw a glorious sight. There was an angel sitting next to the tomb. His clothing was white as snow and his face as bright as lightning! The guards were so afraid that they fainted.

The angel spoke to the women. "Don't be afraid," he said. "You are looking for Jesus, but He is not here. He has risen! Go quickly and tell the others that He has risen from the dead!"

With both fear and excitement, the women left to tell the others what they had seen. On the way, Jesus met them, and they fell at His feet and worshiped Him.

Jesus said, "Do not fear, but go. Tell the others I will meet them in Galilee."

Then with great joy, that is what they did!

» *Matthew 27:57–60, 28:1–10*   » *Luke 23:50–54, 24:1–12*

» *Mark 15:42–46*   » *John 19:38–42*

Jesus Is Alive!

That very night, Jesus appeared to His Apostles in Galilee. As the men were talking together, Jesus suddenly appeared among them. They were both amazed and afraid, and at first they thought they were seeing a spirit.

Jesus said, "Why are you afraid? Why do you doubt? See the holes in my hands and my feet? Go ahead and touch Me and you will see that I am not a ghost. Peace be with you."

"Is this really the Lord?" they wondered. Yet He was standing right next to them. They saw His wounds with their own eyes. He even ate with them. It was Jesus! They were filled with joy and with wonder, and they worshiped Him.

Then He said, *All authority in heaven and on earth has been given to me. Go therefore and make disciples of all nations, baptizing them in the name of the Father and of the Son and of the Holy Spirit, teaching them to observe all that I have commanded you. And behold, I am with you always, to the end of the age* (Matthew 28:18–20).

Now, Thomas was not with the other Apostles when all of this happened, but he joined them after Jesus had left. His friends told him, "Jesus is alive! We have seen Him with our own eyes!"

Thomas did not believe them. "I won't believe it unless I see the nail marks in His hands and touch His side where it was pierced," Thomas said.

Eight days later, the men were meeting again, this time behind locked doors, and Thomas was there. Just as had happened before, Jesus suddenly appeared among them. He looked right at Thomas and said, "Don't doubt, Thomas. Look at My hands and feet and touch My side. Believe!"

"My Lord and my God!" Thomas said in wonder.

Jesus responded, "You believe because you have seen me with your own eyes, but blessed are those who have believed without seeing."

Matthew 28

Mark 16

Luke 24

John 20, 21

The very night after Jesus rose from the dead, He appeared to His Apostles, though they at first thought He must be a spirit. He knew they were afraid, so He held out His hands for them to touch His wounds. The Apostles knew it was Him, and they were filled with joy and worshiped Him. Jesus told them that by His authority they were to make disciples of all nations, to baptize them, and to teach the nations all His truth. Thomas had not been with the Apostles when they saw Jesus and did not yet believe. When Jesus appeared to him, in that moment, he stated, "My Lord and my God!"

Peter Is Restored

Peter had denied Jesus three times on the night of His trial, which gave him much grief and guilt. After a night of fishing, Peter and the others had nothing. A man from the beach asked about this. After telling Him they had caught nothing, the man told them to cast their nets off the other side of the boat. When they did, their nets were overflowing with fish. They knew then that this was Jesus. After they came ashore, Jesus gave them some fish He had cooked. Then Jesus restored Peter and let him know he had an important place in His Church.

Not long after, Peter and some of the others went fishing. They rowed out into the Sea of Galilee and fished until morning, but they didn't catch anything. Not even one fish. So, they headed for the shore.

Now, there was a man standing on the beach. He called out to them, "Did you catch any fish?" They replied. "No."

"Then throw your net to the other side of the boat and you will catch some," he said. Peter and his friends did what the man said, and they caught so many fish they could not haul in the net. Then John said, "It is the Lord!"

When Peter realized it was Jesus, he jumped into the water and swam for shore. The rest of the men followed behind in the boat, dragging their loaded net behind them. Sure enough, Jesus was waiting for them there. He had even cooked breakfast for them.

After they ate, Jesus asked Peter, "Do you love me more than these?" "Yes, Lord," Peter replied. "Then feed my lambs," Jesus said. He asked Peter the same question again. Then again for a third time. Peter was hurt that Jesus asked him again and said, "Lord, you know that I love you!"

God had big plans for Peter. He had been the first one out of all the Apostles to recognize that Jesus was the Messiah, and he would have an important role in the Church going forward. Jesus understood the shame that Peter felt. Peter had once boasted that he would follow Jesus anywhere, even to the point of death. Yet under pressure, he had denied three times that he knew Jesus. He needed to be restored.

Jesus asked Peter the same question three times to give him the opportunity to take back each of his previous denials. Peter's confidence grew as he realized the Lord had forgiven him! His shame was removed as far as the east is from the west, and he was finally ready to give his life in service to the Lord.

John 21:1—19

Thread of Hope

It is not surprising that many religious leaders did not like Jesus. This section began with Him pointing out their greed in contrast to the sacrificial giving of a widow. He had driven the merchants out of the temple. His following was growing by the day. Jesus threatened their way of life.

Just as He had done on the first day of creation, Jesus exposed the darkness that had found its way into the temple. Afterward, the blind and the lame came into the temple. Jesus healed them and He taught them. This was the kind of work that the temple had been made for. Seeing God's work actually being done made the true motives of the religious leaders plain to see, and they hated Jesus for it.

Jesus came as the solution to sin. Human failure had proven that it was the only solution that would work. He offered Himself. The Creator of the world was crucified by the very people He had come to save. Though He was sinless, He willingly took the penalty for the sins of mankind upon Himself. As He hung on that Roman cross, the Savior said, "Father, forgive them, for they know not what they do." What can we say to such love?

Many hundreds of years of religion and thousands upon thousands of animal sacrifices had been unable to accomplish what Jesus did. He was without sin. By His life, He showed us how to live and to love. By His death, He paid the penalty for our sins. By His Resurrection, He proved His power over death and the enemy. Jesus fulfilled the law entirely, and ritual sacrifices would no longer be needed. *Unlike those other high priests, he does not need to offer sacrifices every day. They did this for their own sins first and then for the sins of the people. But Jesus did this once for all when he offered himself as the sacrifice for the people's sins* (Hebrews 7:27; NLT).

The promise in the Garden has been fulfilled (Genesis 3:15).

Adam's disobedience resulted in death for mankind, both spiritually and physically. Christ's obedience offers redemption and everlasting life. His death was not the end of His ministry. It was a new beginning, one filled with a twofold hope:

- All who repent and place their faith in Christ will have their sin debt canceled. They will have the promise of living with their Savior forever in heaven.

- Those who repent also have the promise of living with Him now, in this life. When the veil in the temple that separated mankind from God was torn, the direct access to God that had been lost in the Garden of Eden was restored. The physical temple was no longer necessary. Instead, the Holy Spirit of God would come and dwell in the heart of each believer. The people of God would become the temple (dwelling place of God; 1 Corinthians 3:16–17), and Jesus would be their High Priest (Hebrews 10:19–22).

His Kingdom is real. It exists "already and not yet" — fully in heaven, but also in the hearts, minds, and actions of His followers on earth now. Christians are to live according to the principles of God's Kingdom and not the kingdom of the world, just like the poor widow who gave all that she had. Her offering seemed small by the world's standards, but God saw the heart behind it and was pleased.

ob·sta·cle | something that is in the way of, or blocks a path

One Last Time

The last time the Apostles saw Jesus was in Jerusalem. During this visit, He spent many hours helping them understand the Scriptures and how everything that had been written about Him had been fulfilled. Finally, He said,

"It was written long ago that the Messiah would die and rise again on the third day. It was also written that this message would be preached to all the world: 'There is forgiveness of sins for all who repent.' Now stay here in this city until the Holy Spirit comes and fills you with power. After that, you will be my witnesses in Jerusalem, Judea, and Samaria. Then go into all the world and tell everyone this good news. Whoever believes and is baptized will be saved. Those who refuse to believe will not be saved."

Soon after He spoke these words, Jesus was taken up to heaven. It happened as He lifted His hands to bless the Apostles. After they saw the Lord ascend into the clouds, they worshiped Him. Then they returned to Jerusalem with hearts full of joy and wonder.

The Jews had been waiting on a new king for a long time, yet Jesus had not been the king they expected. Nor had He acted like the king they thought they wanted. Actually, everything He did was unexpected. Jesus was generous and humble. He made time for others. He truly loved everyone, and He called them to live a better life.

His death had sent a wave of sadness and fear through His followers. Nevertheless, their heartache was soon replaced with an unimaginable joy. They finally understood that Jesus was Lord of both heaven and earth. He had conquered sin and death for their sakes. They would see Him again one day.

He had taught them how to be a part of His Kingdom even as they lived on the earth. Now, it was their turn to teach others. There were seeds to plant.

Mark 16:19–20

Luke 24:50–53

Acts 1:8–9

After His Resurrection, Jesus spent His time teaching the Apostles. He helped them understand the Scriptures and how His life and ministry were found throughout God's Word. Then He told them to wait in Jerusalem for the Holy Spirit to fill them with power. After this, they would take the good news into all the world. Then Jesus blessed the Apostles and was taken up into heaven before their eyes. They remembered how sad they were when He died. When He rose from the dead, they had a joy that would never cease. Soon they would be taking this message to every nation.

A Roaring Wind

It was soon time for the Festival of Harvest, also known as Pentecost. This annual holiday was observed 50 days after Passover, and many people were in Jerusalem to celebrate. Some of them had been in town since Passover and had witnessed the crucifixion of Jesus.

Jesus' followers were also there. They were meeting together in someone's home when the most amazing thing happened. The sound of a roaring wind filled the house. Then, what appeared to be flames appeared and settled on each person there. They were filled with the Holy Spirit and began to speak in different languages! Languages they had never spoken before.

They made such a noise that the people outside could hear them and came running from all directions to see what was happening. So, the Apostles went out and began to speak to them about the wonderful things God had done. Much to their amazement, every person heard the message in their native tongue! "How can this be?" they asked. "We are here from over a dozen different countries — and yet we each hear our own language!"

Then Peter stepped forward and said, "Please listen! The Holy Spirit of God has given us the ability to speak to you so that you can understand that the plan of God has been fulfilled. Jesus of Nazareth performed many miracles and signs to prove that He was sent by God, but you rejected Him and had Him killed. Now, He has poured out His Spirit on us so that you might believe. We are here to tell you that Jesus has risen from the dead! God did not allow His Holy One to rot in the grave. We have seen Him with our own eyes. We have heard Him speak. Now, He sits in the place of honor at God's right hand. May everyone in Israel know that this man you crucified is both Lord and Messiah!"

 Acts 2

It had been 50 days since the Apostles had shared their last Passover with Jesus. The time had come for the Festival of Harvest, also known as Pentecost. Jerusalem was filled with Jewish people who had come to celebrate from many nations. Many of Jesus' followers were there praying. A sound like a roaring wind filled the room they were in, and what looked like flames burned above each of them. Then they were filled with the Holy Spirit and began to speak in different languages. A crowd gathered outside, hearing their own languages spoken. Soon, Peter was preaching the good news to the crowd.

Many Were Saved

When the people heard Peter's words, they were very sad. "What can we do?" they asked.

"Repent of your sins and turn to God, and be baptized in the name of Jesus. Then you will also receive the gift of the Holy Spirit," Peter said. Around 3,000 people believed Peter's message. They all repented and were baptized that very day. This is how the Church began to grow.

The new believers were devoted to each other. They shared meals together, they prayed together, and they listened to the teaching of the Apostles. They shared what they had with everyone in the community. They even sold their own belongings so they could help the poor among them. Their joy was contagious, and each day, the Lord added many new believers to their fellowship.

At this time, believers still went to the temple every day to worship and pray. One day, as Peter and John were approaching the temple, they noticed a man who had been born lame. He sat by the gate each day so he could beg from the people going in, and he asked Peter and John for some money.

"I don't have any money to give you," Peter said. "But, I will give you what I do have. In the name of Jesus Christ, get up and walk!" Then he took the man by the hand and helped him to his feet. The man's feet and legs were instantly healed, and he began to walk and jump around, praising God. He entered the temple, and many people saw him walking on his own two feet. They knew this was the lame man they had seen at the temple gate every day for years, and here he was walking around. It was amazing!

Peter seized the opportunity and taught them about Jesus and how all the Scriptures had been fulfilled through Him. Many more people believed. Now there were over 5,000 members of the church in Jerusalem.

Some of the religious leaders were very unhappy about this. They thought they had dealt with the problem of Jesus when they had Him crucified. Now it appeared His influence had grown. So, they had Peter and John arrested and put into jail while they tried to figure out what to do.

Acts 2, 3, 4:1–4

On the day of Pentecost, Peter had begun preaching the good news. The people knew now that Jesus had been crucified for our sins. They also knew He had risen from the dead. Now they wanted to know what they needed to do to be saved. Peter told them they must turn from their sins and come to God and be baptized in the name of Jesus. On that very day, some 3,000 people believed the message and were saved. The number of believers grew each day as Peter and John taught and healed by God's power. This angered the religious leaders, who put them both in jail.

In Whose Name?

The next day, the council of religious leaders met to discuss what to do with the followers of Jesus. They asked Peter and John, "In whose name or by what power have you done this?"

Peter answered them with the help of the Holy Spirit, "Are we being questioned today because we have helped a crippled man?" he said. "Are you asking how he was healed? Let me say clearly, he was healed by the powerful name of Jesus the Nazarene, the same man you crucified. There is salvation in no other name!"

The council members did not know what to say. This man Peter spoke boldly, yet they knew he had no special training in the Scriptures. The man he had healed stood right there among them. Everyone was praising God because of this miracle, and these leaders feared the whole nation would soon be following this small group of uneducated men. They also realized that if they punished Peter and John, the people would most likely riot. So they ordered them to never again speak or teach in the name of Jesus.

Then Peter and John said, "Who do you think God wants us to obey? You? Or Him?"

The council had no choice but to let the men go. As soon as they were free, they told the other believers what had happened. The entire community prayed together that the Lord would give them great boldness in preaching the truth and that they would demonstrate His miraculous power through signs and wonders in the name of Jesus. After they prayed this prayer, the meeting place shook, and they were all filled with the power of the Holy Spirit.

So, the Apostles continued to preach boldly. They continued to heal the sick and the lame. The church continued to grow. Some of the Jewish priests were even converted.

Many of the leaders were outraged. They had to stop this uprising, even if it meant killing the Apostles. One of their leaders stopped them. "Leave these men alone," he said. "If they are doing these things in their own power, they will soon be exposed. If their power comes from God, you will not be able to stop them. You might even find yourselves fighting against God!"

— *Acts 4, 5, 6*

Peter and John were brought before the Jewish council in Jerusalem and asked in whose name they were working miracles. They said boldly that they healed by the powerful name of Jesus, who had been crucified. Fearing the growing followers of Jesus, the council asked Peter and John to stop preaching about Jesus. Then they released them from jail. They and the other Apostles kept preaching and healing in Jesus' name. One of the Jewish leaders spoke to the others and told them to leave this group alone. If their power truly came from God, no one would be able to stop them.

 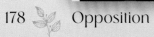

Opposition

The Church was growing rapidly, so the Apostles decided to choose seven men from among them to serve as leaders in the Church. Stephen was one of them. He was full of faith and well respected among the general public. One day, a group of men loyal to the religious leaders plotted against him. They lied to the Jewish High Council, saying that Stephen had spoken against Moses and the temple of God. This was considered a terrible crime, and charges were brought against him.

The high priest asked him, "Are the accusations made against you true?" Stephen gave a brilliant response. He answered by retelling the history of the Jewish nation, starting with Abraham and ending with King Solomon, who built the very temple he was accused of speaking against. Even his worst critics could not disagree with a word he said. Then, he reminded them of the words of Isaiah, who said that God does not live in temples made by human hands.

Finally, Stephen got to the heart of the matter.

"You are stubborn men. Why must you constantly close your ears to the truth and reject the Holy Spirit? Your ancestors persecuted the prophets, and so do you. They even killed the prophets who predicted the coming of the Messiah, the one you betrayed and murdered."

The leaders shook their fists at Stephen. As they did, he gazed up to heaven and said, "Look! I see Jesus standing at God's right hand!"

This infuriated his enemies. Not only had he accused them, but he dared to claim that he had seen God. They had to stop him from spreading this new message. The religion they had known and followed their whole lives was in danger, as were their positions of power and authority. So they dragged Stephen out of the city and stoned him. As they did, he prayed, "Lord Jesus, receive my spirit. Please don't charge these men with this sin."

Stephen died that day, and a great wave of persecution swept over the Church in Jerusalem. Believers were dragged from their homes and sent to prison. Others fled for their lives. One of the men who chased them down was named Saul, a young man from Tarsus.

≫ *Acts 6, 7, 8:1–3*

≫ *Isaiah 66:1–2*

As the Church grew, the Apostles chose seven men who were full of faith to serve as leaders. One of them was named Stephen. A group loyal to the religious leaders began to speak lies against Stephen. They also brought false charges against him to the Jewish High Council. The council asked if what was said against him was true, and his response amazed them. When he told them that they had betrayed and murdered the Messiah, they became furious. They grabbed Stephen, took him out of the city, and killed him with heavy stones. Soon the lives of all believers were in danger.

To Samaria and Beyond

As believers were forced out of the city, they took the good news of Jesus with them. Philip was one of the seven leaders who had been chosen to serve the Church in Jerusalem. He went to Samaria where he performed miracles, cast out evil spirits, and healed the sick, in addition to preaching the good news of Jesus. Many people in Samaria listened and believed, and Peter and John went there to help teach and encourage them.

After they arrived, Philip headed toward Gaza in the south. Along the way, he met the royal treasurer of Ethiopia, who had been visiting Jerusalem. He was seated in a carriage and reading aloud from the Book of Isaiah:

He was oppressed, and he was afflicted,
yet he opened not his mouth;
like a lamb that is led to the slaughter,
and like a sheep that before its shearers is silent,
so he opened not his mouth.
By oppression and judgment he was taken away;
and as for his generation, who considered
that he was cut off out of the land of the living,
stricken for the transgression of my people? (Isaiah 53:7–8).

Philip asked the man, "Do you understand what you are reading?"

"No, because I have no one to help me," the man replied. So Philip began to teach him all that the Scriptures said about the Messiah. Then he told him about Jesus. As they rode along, they came across a small body of water, and the Ethiopian asked Philip to baptize him. Afterward, he was so full of joy! He no doubt took the good news of Jesus all the way back to Ethiopia.

➳ *Acts 8:26–40*

Jerusalem had become very dangerous for believers. So, Philip, another of the seven leaders, left there and took the good news to Samaria. There he preached, performed miracles, cast out evil spirits, and healed those who were sick. Next, he walked toward Gaza and he came across a man in a carriage reading from the Book of Isaiah. This man was the royal treasurer of Ethiopia. Philip asked if the man understood the passage about a man led like a lamb to be killed. When he said he did not, Philip took time to explain these Scriptures about Jesus and was soon baptizing the Ethiopian man.

Eyes to See

Meanwhile, Saul was doing his best to destroy "the Way," which was the name that had been given to this new religion. He went to the High Priest in Jerusalem and requested letters, asking the Jewish leaders in Damascus to cooperate in the capture and arrest of anyone who followed the Way. He planned to bring them back to Jerusalem in chains. There, they would face prison and possible execution.

As he was traveling to Damascus, a light from heaven surrounded Saul. It was so bright that he fell to his knees. Then he heard a voice saying, "Saul! Saul! Why are you persecuting me?" Saul responded, "Who are you?"

"I am the one you are persecuting. I am Jesus. Get up and go to Damascus, and you will be told what to do next," the voice said.

The men who were traveling with Saul were speechless. They had heard the voice — but they had seen no one other than Saul. When Saul got up off the ground, he was totally blind. He could not see a thing. So they led him to Damascus by the hand. He stayed there for three days without eating or drinking.

Now, there was a man who lived in Damascus named Ananias. He was a follower of the Way and one of the people Saul had hoped to arrest. The Lord appeared to Ananias in a vision and told him to go and find Saul and lay hands on him to heal his blindness. "Lord!" Ananias said. "I have heard about this man. He is coming to arrest us."

"Go anyway," the Lord said. "For Saul is my chosen vessel. He will take the good news to the people of Israel, and also to the Gentiles."

So, Ananias did what the Lord said. He found Saul and laid his hands on him. "The Lord Jesus has sent me that you might regain your sight and be filled with the Holy Spirit," he said. Immediately, something like scales fell off of Saul's eyes. Then he was baptized and began to preach about Jesus, saying, "He is indeed the Son of God!"

Saul turned out to be such a powerful preacher that the religious leaders in Damascus plotted to kill him. They set a trap for him at the city gate and watched for him to pass by. So one night, some of the believers lowered him in a basket through a window in the wall of the city and he escaped.

Acts 9:1–25

This new way of believing became known as "the Way." Saul, a Jewish leader, was wanting to hunt down and arrest all those who followed the Way. On the road to Damascus, a bright light from heaven shown down on him, and he heard a voice asking, "Why are you persecuting me?" Saul, who was blinded by the light, asked who this was, and the voice told him this was Jesus. Jesus then directed Saul to go to Damascus and wait. There, a follower of Jesus named Ananias came to him, healed him, and directed him to begin speaking the good news of Jesus.

Peter and Cornelius

There was a man named Cornelius who was a Gentile. He was also an officer in the Roman army, and he was a good man. He was one of the few Gentiles who were accepted by the Jews because he had converted to Judaism at some point in his life. He gave to the poor and prayed to God regularly. One afternoon, he had a vision where an angel of God spoke to him. "Cornelius! Your prayers and good works have been received by God," he said. "Now, send for my servant Peter and ask him to come to your home."

So Cornelius called two of his servants and sent them to find Peter. Meanwhile, Peter had gone up to a rooftop to pray. It was lunchtime, and Peter was hungry. While he was praying, he had a vision of a large sheet of cloth coming down from heaven. Inside the cloth were all kinds of animals that were forbidden to be eaten under Jewish law. He heard a voice say, "Wake up, Peter. Kill and eat these animals."

"I have never eaten any food forbidden by our Jewish laws," Peter said. The vision was repeated three times, and the voice said, "Do not call something unclean if God has made it clean."

As Peter was wondering about the meaning of his vision, Cornelius' servants arrived and asked him to come with them to the home of their master. When they arrived, they found Cornelius' house full of people waiting to hear a message from Peter. Peter said, "As you know, it is against our laws for a Jewish man to enter the home of a Gentile. Even so, God has shown me that it is wrong to think of another person as unclean. For God will accept people from every nation who fear Him and do what is right. This is the message God has for you — there is peace with God through Jesus Christ, the Messiah. He was put to death on the Cross, but God raised Him back to life. He has told us to preach the good news that He lives and that He is the Lord of heaven and earth. Everyone who repents and believes on His name will have their sins forgiven."

They believed his message and received the Holy Spirit, which amazed the Jewish visitors who had traveled with Peter. It was clear to everyone that the good news was not just for the Jews but for all people. The new believers were baptized, and Peter stayed to teach and encourage them for several days.

Acts 10

Cornelius was a Roman officer. Many people looked down on him because he was a Gentile, though he had converted to Judaism. God gave Cornelius a vision of an angel who told him to send for Peter. Peter also had a vision; he saw a cloth being lowered from heaven, filled with animals forbidden for Jews to eat. God said, "Do not call anything impure that God has made clean" (Acts 10:15). Peter wondered what his vision meant. When he learned that Cornelius wanted him to come into his home and teach about Jesus, he understood. Peter realized that the good news of Jesus was not just for the Jews. It was for everyone.

The Church in Antioch

After this, believers began to actively seek out Gentiles to tell them about the good news of Jesus. In Antioch, a city in Syria, a large number of Gentiles turned to the Lord. So Barnabas went there to teach them, and he asked Saul (whose Roman name was Paul) to join him.

Antioch was one of the largest cities in the Roman Empire. It was a prosperous city, located near Egypt, Asia Minor, Greece, Italy, and Mesopotamia. This made it a popular stopping point for travelers and made it possible for people from other countries to hear Paul and Barnabas share the good news of Jesus. These men stayed there for an entire year, teaching and encouraging everyone who believed. It was there that followers of the Way were first called Christians.

One day, a believer named Agabus predicted that a famine was going to come upon the entire Roman world. So the church in Antioch took up a collection to help the Christians who would be impacted by the famine. Then they sent the money to the church in Judea.

The church at Antioch was made up of people from different races and economic abilities. Yet they were united in their beliefs and actions. They worshiped together regularly, helped other believers around the empire, and sent out missionaries to spread the gospel to other parts of the world. In so doing, they set a fine example for other churches that is still being followed to this day.

Acts 11:19–30

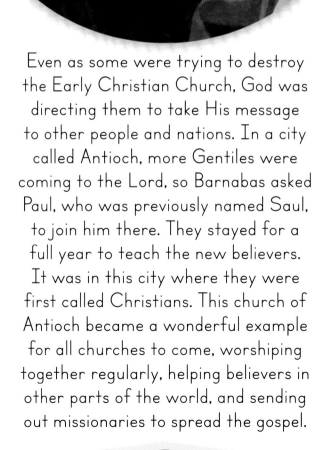

Even as some were trying to destroy the Early Christian Church, God was directing them to take His message to other people and nations. In a city called Antioch, more Gentiles were coming to the Lord, so Barnabas asked Paul, who was previously named Saul, to join him there. They stayed for a full year to teach the new believers. It was in this city where they were first called Christians. This church of Antioch became a wonderful example for all churches to come, worshiping together regularly, helping believers in other parts of the world, and sending out missionaries to spread the gospel.

Thread of Hope

The religious leaders had thought Jesus' death would put an end to the Way. That had not happened. In fact, Christianity was spreading. Though they tried, the religious leaders were powerless to stop it.

The Christians found that living according to God's Kingdom brought a mixture of joy and hardship, purpose and pain. Yet they persevered. They realized that the struggles they faced could not take away from the joy they would experience for eternity.

Stephen died praying for those who killed him, just as he had seen Jesus do. In his final moments, God allowed him to see a glimpse of heaven. He saw where he was going and described it out loud for all to hear. What hope this must have given to the other believers who would also face persecution in the days to come!

Paul had been on a mission to find and arrest Christians. He put them in chains and sent them to prison. He had great power and authority, but he was no match for Jesus. His encounter on the road to Damascus left him a changed man. He was blinded by Jesus' light for three days. On the third day God sent a believer named Ananias to restore his sight.

Imagine the confusion and fear Ananias must have felt. God wanted him to help the man who had come to arrest him? Yet he obeyed the Lord. Paul's sight was restored both physically and spiritually. He would go on to share the good news with all who would listen. Paul had an incredible impact on the Church and wrote a good portion of the New Testament. What would have happened if Ananias had acted out of fear instead of obedience?

Meanwhile, the persecution that had begun in Jerusalem served to help spread the gospel further. As the believers fled, they took the good news with them throughout Judea and Samaria. The Church was growing by leaps and bounds in that region. Jesus had told His Apostles to carry the gospel to the ends of the earth. So they began to share the good news in other parts of the world as well.

This story continues today. We live in a time known as the Church Age, or the age of the Great Commission. Like the church in Antioch, Christians still meet together in communities to worship God and study His Word. Although many believers around the world still suffer persecution, Christians are still bringing the light of Christ into the dark places they encounter.

This is the mission of the Church until Christ returns.

Pen·te·cost	a Christian holiday celebrating the arrival of the Holy Spirit
fel·low·ship	a community of people with common beliefs
mis·sion·ar·y	one who is sent out to teach or to preach
Gen·tile	a person who is not Jewish
per·se·cu·tion	mistreatment of people based on their beliefs or ethnicity

Touched by an Angel

Back in Jerusalem, King Agrippa I was the king. He was the grandson of Herod the Great and the nephew of Herod Antipas, who ruled in Galilee. In keeping with the family legacy, he was power hungry. In an effort to gain the support of the Jewish people, he persecuted the Christians in Jerusalem. He had the Apostle James (the brother of John) killed and Peter arrested. It was his plan to have a public trial where Peter would most likely have been executed.

Peter was put in chains and under heavy guard, but the Church prayed earnestly for his safety. The night before he was to stand trial, an angel appeared in his cell. He touched Peter and told him, "Hurry and get up. Then follow me closely!" Peter's chains fell off of him.

Then he followed the angel out of the cell. He thought he was having a dream as they passed by one set of guards and then another. No one noticed them! Finally, they came to the gate leading to the city. The gate opened on its own, and they passed through to freedom. It was then that the angel left — and Peter realized it had not been a dream after all.

He hurried over to Mary's house, where all the believers had gathered to pray for him. He told them how the Lord had sent an angel to rescue him.

"Tell the others what has happened," Peter said. Then he left.

The next morning, the prison was in an uproar. The soldiers could not explain what had happened because none of them had seen anything. Herod Agrippa ordered a thorough search of the grounds, but Peter could not be found. He was so angry that he sentenced the guards to death.

Not long after this, an angel of the Lord struck Herod Agrippa with a terrible illness, and he died.

The gospel continued to spread.

Acts 13, 14

To fight the growing Church, Herod Agrippa I, the power-hungry ruler in Jerusalem, began to capture and kill the followers of Jesus. It was at this time that Peter was arrested and put in chains surrounded by many guards. It was also at this time that the Church was praying for Peter's safety. The night before his trial, an angel appeared to him. The angel touched him and told him to come outside. As Peter got up, his chains fell off, and he walked through the prison. He was soon running to Mary's house. Everyone there knew their prayers had been answered. Soon after, Herod Agrippa died of a terrible illness.

Paul's First Missionary Journey

The church in Antioch appointed Paul and Barnabas as missionaries and sent them out to spread the gospel. They sailed first for the island of Cyprus. They preached from town to town across the island. From there, they traveled by ship to Pamphylia, and from there to Pisidia, where they taught in the local synagogue. Word spread throughout the city that these men were teaching a new message. On the next Sabbath, it seemed as if the entire city showed up to hear them speak. Some of the religious leaders began to argue against what Paul and Barnabas were teaching.

Paul and Barnabas replied by saying, "We presented the good news first to the Jews. Since you refuse to accept it, we will present it to the Gentiles because that is what the Lord instructed us to do."

The Gentiles believed the message of the gospel, and their hearts were filled with joy to know that they were loved and chosen by God. The Jews who were against Paul and Barnabas stirred up a mob of people who ran them out of the city. So they shook the dust from their feet as they left. They went to Iconium, and the same thing happened there. While some of the Jews believed the good news, others stirred the people up against them. When they learned that a group of people planned to attack them, the two men fled to the Lycaonian region of Galatia.

There, they preached the gospel and healed a man who had been lame since birth. When the local people heard about the miracle, they decided that the missionaries must be gods. The people prepared to offer sacrifices to them. Paul and Barnabas stopped them, saying, "Don't do this! We are men just like you. We have come to tell you to turn from these false gods and turn instead to Jesus." Then some Jews arrived and stoned Paul until they thought he was dead. After they left, Paul got up and went back to town. The next day, he and Barnabas left for Derbe.

After preaching in Derbe, they risked their lives and returned to each town where people had turned to God. They encouraged all of the new Christians and appointed elders in every church that had sprung up. With prayer and fasting, they trusted these new churches to the care of the Lord. Then they returned to Antioch and told the believers all that had happened on their journey. They stayed there for some time, resting from their travels.

Acts 14

Paul and Barnabas were sent out as missionaries from the church in Antioch. They took the good news to Cyprus, Pamphylia, and Pisidia. As they taught in one of the synagogues there, the religious leaders began to argue with them. Though the Gentiles accepted the message with joy, the Jewish leaders gathered a mob to chase Paul and Barnabas away. They realized that the Lord was calling them to the Gentiles. They continued to share the gospel. Some became believers, while others attacked them, even nearly stoning Paul to death. Then Paul and Barnabas returned to Antioch to tell of their journey.

Paul's Second Missionary Journey

After some time, Paul prepared to go on another journey. This time, he chose Silas to go with him. First, they traveled to the churches that Paul and Barnabas had previously planted to encourage the believers there. Then they went throughout Galatia, spreading the good news in every town and village they came across.

One night, Paul had a vision of a man from Macedonia asking them to come and help them. Timothy, a young believer, wanted to go along. Soon the three men sailed across the Aegean Sea for the distant land of Macedonia.

After they arrived, they met up with a group of Jewish women in Philippi. One of them was named Lydia. She believed the gospel and was baptized along with her entire household. After Lydia's conversion, she invited the three men to stay in her home.

From there, they traveled to Thessalonica, where they stayed for some time. As usual, there were some who believed and others who stirred up trouble against them. Their enemies began to claim that they were guilty of treason against Caesar, which was a very serious crime. "These men have been causing trouble all over the world," they said. "And now they are trying to cause problems here as well."

So, Paul and Silas left for Berea. The people there were more open to the gospel, and many believed. Some Jews from Thessalonica soon arrived to work against them. So, they moved on to Athens, where Paul preached for some time. Many of the people in Athens laughed at his message, but a few believed.

Next, they went to Corinth. Paul testified in the Jewish synagogue about Jesus, though many Jewish people there opposed him. Nevertheless, many Gentiles in Corinth did believe, so Paul stayed there for over a year, teaching and encouraging the church that formed there.

Finally, after traveling many miles and planting many churches, Paul returned to Antioch.

Acts 15:36–41, 16–18

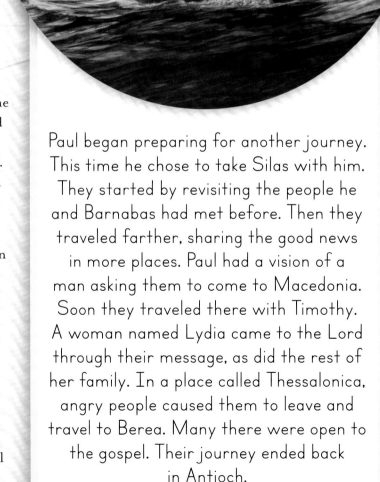

Paul began preparing for another journey. This time he chose to take Silas with him. They started by revisiting the people he and Barnabas had met before. Then they traveled farther, sharing the good news in more places. Paul had a vision of a man asking them to come to Macedonia. Soon they traveled there with Timothy. A woman named Lydia came to the Lord through their message, as did the rest of her family. In a place called Thessalonica, angry people caused them to leave and travel to Berea. Many there were open to the gospel. Their journey ended back in Antioch.

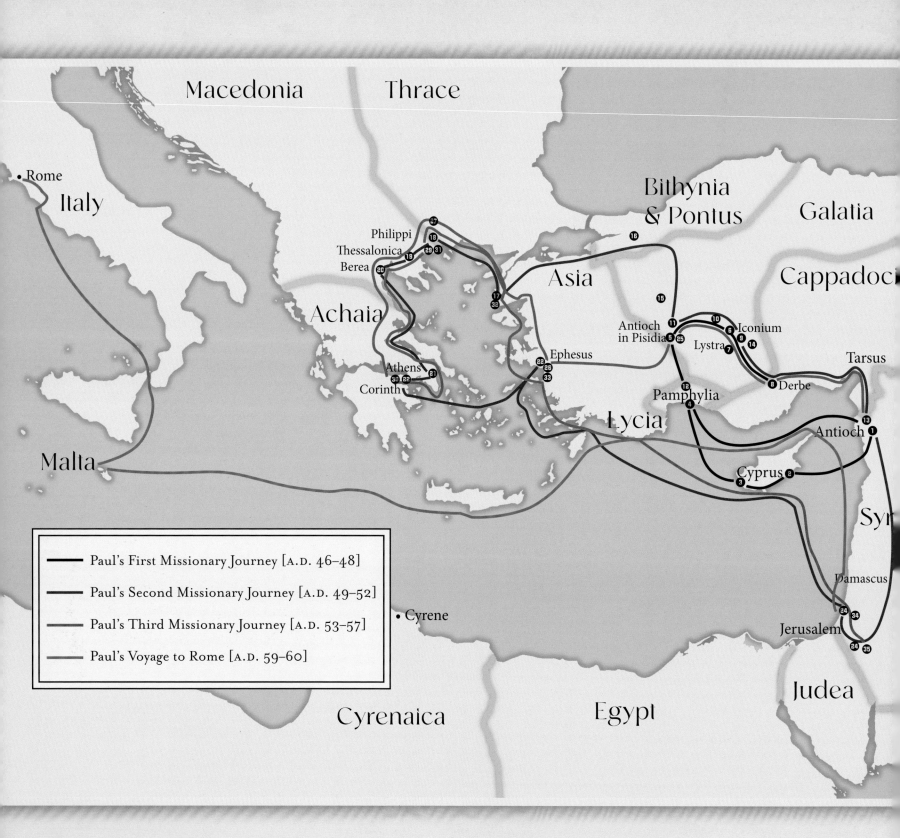

Macedonia

Thrace

Bithynia & Pontus

Galatia

Cappadoci

Asia

Rome

Italy

Achaia

Philippi
Thessalonica
Berea

Athens
Corinth

Ephesus

Lycia

Pamphylia

Antioch
in Pisidia

Iconium

Lystra

Derbe

Tarsus

Antioch

Cyprus

Syr

Damascus

Malta

Jerusalem

Judea

——— Paul's First Missionary Journey [A.D. 46–48]

——— Paul's Second Missionary Journey [A.D. 49–52]

——— Paul's Third Missionary Journey [A.D. 53–57]

——— Paul's Voyage to Rome [A.D. 59–60]

Cyrene

Cyrenaica

Egypt

Paul's Third Missionary Journey

After resting for a while, Paul set out again. This time he traveled to Ephesus, where he found people who had already heard the good news. A man named Apollos had previously traveled through the area and had taught them about Jesus. They had not been baptized, so Paul baptized them in the name of Jesus, and they received the gift of the Holy Spirit.

He taught there for two years. Ephesus was a popular city for travelers, who often went to the lecture hall when they were in town. Many people from throughout the province of Asia had the opportunity to hear the gospel message during the time that Paul was there.

Now, there was a man named Demetrius who lived in Ephesus. He had a successful business selling idols, and his business had suffered because so many people were becoming Christians. He rallied the local community against Paul, and a riot started. So, Paul decided to go to Macedonia.

Paul and his traveling companions spent several months traveling through Macedonia and Greece and then planned to go to Jerusalem. Paul wanted to get there in time for the Festival of Pentecost. Along the way, they stopped near Ephesus, and Paul sent for the leaders of the church.

"The Holy Spirit is leading me to Jerusalem," he told them, "and while I don't know what will happen to me there, I do know that jail and suffering will be in my future. My life is worthless if I don't finish the work the Lord has given me to do, and that is to preach the necessity of repenting from sin and turning to the Lord Jesus. Now, I entrust you to God. You must watch out for false teachers after I leave and remain true to what you have been taught."

The Ephesian church leaders prayed with Paul before he and his companions embarked on their journey to Jerusalem. Paul was able to meet with other believers along the way. Many times, the believers they met with urged Paul not to go to Jerusalem. They were afraid for him, but Paul was determined to obey the Holy Spirit.

Acts 19, 20, 21:1–14

Paul was soon ready to travel a third time. He went to Ephesus and found that many there had already believed in Jesus, but they had not been baptized. So Paul baptized them, and they received the gift of the Holy Spirit. He taught the people in Ephesus for two years. Demetrius, a local man who sold idols, was upset because Paul's teaching was hurting his business. He stirred up trouble, and Paul ended up leaving town. He later stopped at a nearby city and was able to talk to his friends from Ephesus again. He told them that God had called him to Jerusalem. Though dangerous, he would follow God's plan.

Prison for Paul

Paul made his way back to Jerusalem. He knew there were people there who hated him, but he trusted God to guide his way. When he arrived, he shared what God had done on his missionary journeys. Soon the religious leaders found Paul and had him arrested. Then they planned to kill him. The Roman officer guarding him discovered their plan and had Paul moved to Caesarea to keep him safe. Paul was kept in prison there for two years, but he was treated kindly. He even shared the good news of Jesus with the governor of Caesarea.

When Paul arrived in Jerusalem, he met with James (the brother of Jesus) and the other leaders of the city's church. Paul encouraged them by telling them of all that God had done as he preached the gospel to the Gentiles over the last several years. One by one, he told them about each new church that had been planted.

After hearing Paul's news, the men rejoiced and told him that many thousands of Jews had also become believers while he had been away. The good news of Jesus was spreading, and the religious leaders in Jerusalem were not happy about it.

It did not take long for them to hear that Paul was in town. They soon had him arrested on religious charges. The next day, a Roman commander took Paul to appear before the Jewish High Council, but the council was divided about what to do. The leaders began to argue among themselves — some of them found no fault with Paul, and others wanted him dead. The conflict grew so violent that the Roman commander ordered Paul to be taken back to jail.

Paul had a dream that night where the Lord told him not to worry about his situation, for God had plans for Paul to go to Rome and preach the gospel there.

The next morning, a group of more than forty Jewish men plotted to kill Paul. They told the High Council to request that Paul be brought to stand before them again; only this time, these men planned to ambush and kill him along the way.

The Roman commander heard about their plot and sent Paul under heavy guard to the city of Caesarea for his protection. Five days later, some of the Jewish leaders from Jerusalem arrived in Caesarea and pressed charges against Paul. Paul and his accusers were taken before the governor of Caesarea, whose name was Felix. Felix listened to both sides and postponed Paul's hearing for another date. Paul was kept in prison at Herod's headquarters in Caesarea for another two years, but he was treated kindly. He was allowed visitors and even met with the governor and his wife Drusilla several times, telling them the good news of Jesus.

Acts 21–25

Paul Speaks to the King

After two years, a man named Festus replaced Felix as governor of Caesarea. The religious leaders wasted no time trying to convince this new governor to have Paul transferred back to Jerusalem. Their desire to kill Paul had not diminished in the two years he had been held in Caesarea.

Festus refused their request. "If you want to accuse Paul of a crime, you must do it in Caesarea," he said. That is what they did. Around a week later, Paul and his accusers stood before Festus. The leaders made accusations against Paul, but they had no proof he had done anything wrong.

Festus asked Paul if he was willing to return to Jerusalem to stand trial. Paul replied, "No! I am a Roman citizen, and I want to be tried in a Roman court. Everyone here knows that I am innocent, and you know that if I am sent to Jerusalem, I will be killed. I appeal to Caesar!" Paul felt safer leaving his fate to a Gentile than to the religious leaders of Jerusalem.

So, Paul was kept in prison in Caesarea until he could be sent to Rome to appear before Caesar. A few days later, King Agrippa II of Jerusalem arrived in Caesarea with his sister, Bernice, to visit the new governor. When he learned about what had happened between the Jewish leaders and Paul, he wanted to hear Paul's side of the story.

"You may speak in your defense," the king said. Paul told the king that he had been raised and well-educated in Jerusalem, and that, as a young man, he strongly opposed the Christians. Then Paul told him about his experience on the road to Damascus and all that had happened since.

"My message," he said, "to both Jews and Gentiles, is to repent and turn to God. I teach the same thing that the prophets did, that the Messiah would suffer and die, and be the first to rise from the dead. He did these things to save us from our sins. I pray to God that everyone here would believe this good news."

Then King Agrippa said to the governor, "This man has done nothing to deserve imprisonment." Despite the king's opinion, Roman law required that Paul stand trial before Caesar.

Acts 25—26

Just after two years, a man named Festus became governor of Caesarea. The religious leaders tried to convince the new governor to send Paul to Jerusalem, but Festus refused. A hearing was held in Caesarea, and Festus asked Paul if he was willing to go to Jerusalem for trial. Paul refused and appealed to Caesar instead. King Agrippa II and Bernice came to hear Paul's defense, in which he explained that he preached repentance and faith in the Messiah who had suffered and died for our sins and rose from the dead. The king declared Paul innocent, but Roman law required he stand trial before Caesar.

Shipwrecked

Eventually, Paul and several other prisoners were put aboard a ship for Rome. They encountered strong winds that made sailing difficult, and they lost a lot of time. The captain and his men decided to try and make it to Phoenix, a city off the coast of Crete, so they could spend the winter there. Before long, the weather became more fierce. Hurricane force winds battered the ship. The crew was frightened and began throwing their cargo overboard. The storm raged for several days until the men lost all hope. No one had eaten anything for days, when Paul said, "Be strong. For last night an angel of the God I serve told me not to be afraid. We will be shipwrecked for a time, but no one here is going to die in this storm!"

Then he urged everyone to eat. He took some bread and, after thanking God for it, began to eat it. Then the other 276 people on the ship ate some also. The next morning, they spotted land and decided to try and run the ship aground. The ship broke apart on the rocks, and they had to swim for it. Just as Paul had said, every person on the ship survived.

They were on the island of Malta, where they spent the next three months. While they were there, Paul shared the good news and healed the sick. As a result, the people of Malta supplied all of their needs while they were on the island, and also when they set sail on a new ship the next spring.

They finally arrived in Rome. The Christians who lived there had heard they were coming, and they came out to greet Paul, which encouraged him greatly. Paul was treated kindly by the Roman officers in charge of him. Even though he was still a prisoner, he was allowed to have his own home.

Three days after he arrived, he called together the local Jewish leaders and told them why he had been arrested. Then a large crowd gathered at his home, and Paul told them the good news of Jesus. He taught from the law of Moses and the books of the prophets from daybreak to sunset. Some people were persuaded by his words, but others refused to believe. To them, Paul said,

The Holy Spirit was right in saying to your fathers through Isaiah the prophet: 'Go to this people, and say, "You will indeed hear but never understand, and you will indeed see but never perceive." For this people's heart has grown dull, and with their ears they can barely hear, and their eyes they have closed; lest they should see with their eyes and hear with their ears and understand with their heart and turn, and I would heal them.' Therefore let it be known to you that this salvation of God has been sent to the Gentiles; they will listen (Acts 28:25–28).

Paul spent the next two years in Rome, boldly proclaiming the gospel to all who would listen.

≫ *Acts 27–28*

To transport them to Rome, Paul and some other prisoners were loaded onto a ship. It was not long before a powerful storm rose up, and the crew was filled with fear. An angel had come to Paul in the night. Paul shared that the angel had told him the ship would be destroyed, but no one on it would die. He had everyone eat so they stayed strong. The next morning, the ship broke apart, and everyone swam to an island called Malta. Paul preached and healed the sick there for three months. Then they finally went on to Rome. He would spend two years in Rome telling others of the gospel.

Paul's Letters and Legacy

*P*aul wrote a lot of letters during his career as a missionary. He wrote to his friends and his students. He also wrote to the churches he had planted.

Paul often preached to individuals and groups of people to instruct them in biblical truth. When he was away from them, he often wrote them letters. Many of Paul's letters are now part of the Bible. These letters, sometimes called epistles, were meant to encourage and to instruct others in the Christian faith. Though Paul faced being stoned, beaten, and thrown in prison, his strong faith helped ensure that God's Word would still be available to guide us today.

The books of Romans, 1 Corinthians, 2 Corinthians, Galatians, Ephesians, Philippians, Colossians, 1 Thessalonians, 2 Thessalonians, 1 Timothy, 2 Timothy, Titus, and Philemon were all letters written by Paul. Some (Ephesians, Philippians, Colossians, and Philemon) were written from his prison cell.

Paul's letters are rich with sound teaching. As with all the other books of the Bible, they were written under the inspiration of the Holy Spirit. They help us understand the history and culture of the time. More importantly, they offer instruction on both the simple and deeper truths of the Christian faith.

Paul suffered being stoned, whipped, and from spending several years of his life in prison in order to fulfill the calling God had put on his life. It can be hard to understand why he had to endure so much hardship, but a big picture view allows us to see that those circumstances gave him the opportunity to share the good news with people he would not ordinarily speak with — like fellow prisoners, Roman soldiers, and dignitaries. He even witnessed to a king.

Paul is quoted as saying, *But I do not account my life of any value nor as precious to myself, if only I may finish my course and the ministry that I received from the Lord Jesus, to testify to the gospel of the grace of God (Acts 20:24).*

As he finished his course, Christianity spread throughout the Roman Empire and beyond. Believers today are still reaping the benefits of Paul's obedience to the gospel and faithfulness to God. His love for the Lord and for people were evident throughout his Christian life and the letters he wrote. He clearly took the words of Jesus to heart:

"This is my commandment, that you love one another as I have loved you. Greater love has no one than this, that someone lay down his life for his friends" (John 15:12–13).

Romans	Philippians	2 Timothy
1 Corinthians	Colossians	Titus
2 Corinthians	1 Thessalonians	Philemon
Galatians	2 Thessalonians	
Ephesians	1 Timothy	

Other Important Letters

*L*etters were an important means of communication for the Early Church. Traveling to another city was neither fast nor easy in those days. Yet, the gospel was spreading. Churches were popping up around the Roman Empire. These letters served to encourage, educate, and challenge Christians who lived in various locations.

The letter of Hebrews was written to Jewish Christians who were persecuted and often pressured to return to their old religion. This letter encouraged them to stay strong in their faith and provided proof that Jesus was the Messiah who had been promised in the Jewish Scriptures.

James wrote a very important letter to the Jewish Christians who lived outside of Judea. He reminded them to be doers of the word and not hearers only. Our works cannot save us, but true faith will result in obedience to God's Word and a genuine love for others. He also gave wise advice on facing temptations and the daily struggles of life.

Since they had no phones or computers in the time of the Early Church, the main way people communicated when they were apart was by sending letters. The letters of Paul and others helped to educate and challenge believers in the countries where Christianity was growing. For example, James wrote a letter to Jewish Christians, telling them to live out God's Word, not simply to hear it. Peter wrote several letters to believers in the Roman Empire, often speaking of suffering and trials and how believers could rise above the pain. John also wrote letters that spoke of love and warned of false teachings.

Peter wrote two letters to encourage believers throughout the Roman Empire. Peter was a strong leader who also suffered much for his faith. He wanted others to understand that suffering was a possibility, but that God would not abandon them in their trials. They were to live in light of eternity, where their reward would be great.

Jude wrote on the topic of false teachers. He condemned the false teaching that Christians were free to sin because they were no longer under the law. He encouraged believers to defend the faith and not fall victim to these false teachers.

John wrote three letters addressing the topics of false teaching, Christian fellowship, and the importance of loving one another.

Human nature has not changed. Today's Christian faces the same struggles as the Early Church, which is why these letters are just as true and important today as they were when they were written (2 Timothy 3:16).

— 1 John

— 2 John

— 3 John

— 2 Timothy 3:16

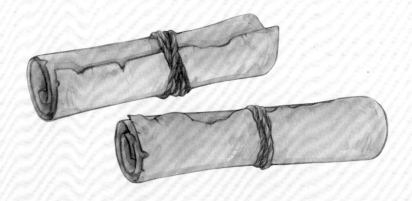

John had been a young man when he walked with Jesus. When he was old, he was exiled to an island named Patmos. While on Patmos, the Lord gave John a vision of what was to come. He wrote down this vision, and it became the last book of the New Testament. It is called the Book of Revelation. First, John spoke messages to the churches with warning and encouragement. Then he shared of God's ultimate triumph to come, when evil would fail, and a new heaven and earth would be a place of peace for all believers.

John's Revelation

By the time the Apostle John was an old man, Christianity had spread throughout the Roman Empire. Every effort to stop it had failed. Nevertheless, enemies of the Church were common. History records the persecution and death of many Christians during this time in history. John's punishment for preaching the gospel was exile. He was banished to Patmos, a remote island off the coast of modern-day Turkey.

Banishment was meant to stop John from having an impact on Christianity. Instead, it had the opposite effect. While he was on the island, John had an amazing vision. He described it in great detail in a letter that would later become known as the Book of Revelation.

I was in the Spirit on the Lord's day, and I heard behind me a loud voice like a trumpet saying, "Write what you see in a book and send it to the seven churches, to Ephesus and to Smyrna and to Pergamum and to Thyatira and to Sardis and to Philadelphia and to Laodicea" (Revelation 1:10–11).

The first part of the vision included messages from Jesus to the Church. Those messages warned and encouraged believers to be ready for His return.

Then the scene shifted as John described God's plan to save His people from Satan.

Thankfully, we are told how the story will end. John's vision included a glimpse of the new heaven and new earth that will come at Christ's return. In this glorious place, God will make a home with His people. There will be no more sin, suffering, or death, for the old order of things will pass away and Satan will be destroyed.

John's vision became the last book in the Bible. It serves as the perfect complement to the first book. Genesis and Revelation are the bookends that hold the rest of the story together.

GENESIS	REVELATION
The earth was created (Genesis 1:1)	The earth passes away (Revelation 21:1)
The sun and moon created (Genesis 1:16)	No need for sun and moon (Revelation 21:23)
Tree of life and river in Eden (Genesis 2:9–10)	Tree of life and river in the new Jerusalem (Revelation 22:1–2)
Marriage of the first Adam (Genesis 2:18)	Marriage of the last Adam (Revelation 16:7)
Satan's first rebellion (Genesis 3:1–6)	Satan's final rebellion (Revelation 3:7–10)
Entrance of sin (Genesis 3:6–7)	End of sin (Revelation 21:27)
Satan's doom announced (Genesis 3:15)	Satan's doom fulfilled (Revelation 20:10)
The Redeemer is promised (Genesis 3:15)	The Redeemer reigns forever (Revelation 21:22)
Pain and suffering as result of sin (Genesis 3:16)	No more pain and suffering (Revelation 21:4)
The ground is cursed (Genesis 3:17)	The curse is done away with (Revelation 22:3)
Entrance of death (Genesis 3:19)	End of death (Revelation 21:4)
Driven from God's presence (Genesis 3:24)	Will see God's face (Revelation 22:4)
Tree of life guarded (Genesis 3:24)	Tree of life available (Revelation 22:14)

Look, I am coming soon! My reward is with me, and I will give to each person according to what they have done. I am the Alpha and the Omega, the First and the Last, the Beginning and the End (Revelation 22:12–13; NIV).

Thread of Hope

Long ago, God made mankind after His own image and gave them a perfect place to dwell. It was a beautiful Garden, a place where they could walk and talk with Him. They were told to care for the Garden and all that God had created.

Their faith was tested when Satan sowed sin in the Garden. Our first parents took that seed and planted it, and a seedling of evil soon sprouted. In time, the harvest came. Pain, sickness, and death multiplied on the earth.

So began this sweeping story of redemption. God is the hero of this story, for without Him, all would have been lost. It took many years for His promise in the Garden to come to pass, but time is a wonderful teacher. During these years, it became clear that mankind did not have the ability to save himself, for all people are tempted to trust their own wisdom instead of trusting God's wisdom.

Throughout this story, God rescued His children from the penalty of sin. He provided the first sacrifice for Adam and Eve. He saved Noah and his family. He provided a ram to take Isaac's place. He accepted the blood of the Passover lamb, and He literally walked with Israel as they left Egypt. The scarlet rope that saved Israel's spies and Rahab's family serves as a visual reminder of God's provision and protection. Later, that thread wove through Israel's sacrificial system.

These sacrifices had to be repeated because they were not sufficient to atone for sin once and for all time. Thankfully, God is faithful even when people are not. He sent His own Son, born as a child of Israel, to fulfill the promise He had made in the Garden. Jesus lived a perfect life, which qualified Him to become the perfect sacrifice. Sin was atoned for once and for all as His precious blood was spilled for all people. The One who had required the first sacrifice offered Himself as the last. *"Behold, the Lamb of God, who takes away the sin of the world!" (John 1:29).*

Jesus conquered death and promised that all who repented and placed their faith in Him would also. They would receive the Holy Spirit and the "new heart" that Ezekiel preached about (Ezekiel 11:19). This is the gospel. It is the life-changing good news of Jesus.

The Apostles took this good news and shared it, and hope began to spread on the earth. The Early Church modeled a devoted Christian life. Their faith and stories have encouraged believers through the ages to hold fast to the Lord. Christians have often felt like strangers in this world, for the world has often been hostile toward them. Many attempts have been made to put an end to Christianity over the years, but the truth and hope of Christ has endured.

One day, Jesus will return for His Church. Satan and his followers will be destroyed for good, and those who have put their faith in the Lord will live forever with Him in a redeemed Kingdom. Until that day comes,

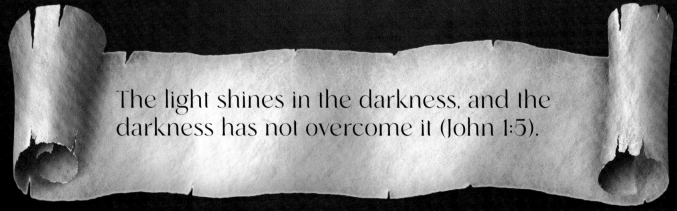

The light shines in the darkness, and the darkness has not overcome it (John 1:5).

Bill Looney

Bill is the visionary talent behind some of the most unique Christian titles available today, creating illustrations in a variety of styles and mediums that bring to life projects like *Dinosaurs for Kids* and *The True Story of Noah's Ark*. He was formally schooled in all media beginning in public school to the University of Texas at Arlington and the Dallas Art Institute. Bill is proficient in all media, ranging from airbrush, oils, acrylics, pen & ink, watercolor, sculpture, and computer illustration.

All illustrations by Bill Looney unless otherwise noted.

Archaeologyillustrated.com: p 40, p 57, p 79, p 98, p 104, p 107, p 114, p 128, p 144, p 172, p 183, p 186, p 187

Goodsalt.com: p 31, p 42, p 70, p 71, p 96, p 110, p 139, p 158, p 177, p 191

Shutterstock.com: p 62, p 66, p 118, p 140, p 150, p 159, p 188, p 195, p 198

istock.com: p 11

Superstock.com: p 28, p 38, p 43, p 48, p 52, p 74, p 80, p 84-85, p 88 left, p 89 left, p 90 left and right, p 92, p 95, p 101, p 105, p 111, p 122, p 154, p 162, p 167, p 170, p 180, p 185,

Wikimedia.com: p 32, p 60, p 89 right, p 141
Images from Wikimedia Commons are used under the CC0 1.0, CC BY-SA 2.0 DE, CC-BY-SA-3.0 license or the GNU Free Documentation License, Version 1.3.

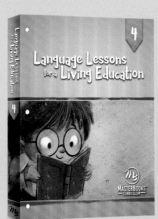
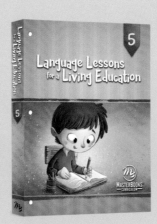